T0369937

Published by Semiotext(e)
PO BOX 629, South Pasadena, CA 91031
www.semiotexte.com

Special thanks to Stella Peacock-Berardini and Robert Dewhurst

Cover Photograph: Lori Hiris
Design: Hedi El Kholti

ISBN: 978-1-63590-251-8

10 9 8 7 6 5 4 3 2 1

Printed and bound in the United States of America.
Distributed by the MIT Press, Cambridge, MA.

Airless Spaces

Shulamith Firestone

Introduction by Chris Kraus
Afterword by Susan Faludi

semiotext(e)

Contents

EXEMPLARY STORIES

"I just keep thinking, Well, I'm twenty-two, what have I done?" Shulamith Firestone told the young documentary filmmakers who followed her around during her last year as a student at the School of the Art Institute of Chicago. It was 1967 and they'd chosen her as an exemplar of the Now Generation. "I want to catch time short and not just drift along with it," she says to her off-camera interviewers. "I want to be a master of time, because it's not enough for me to just live and die." Intense, brilliant, exuberant, and terrified of wasting her life, she was already aware of the marginalization and pressure exerted by men on "any intellectual woman or woman involved in the arts." The film was called *Shulie* and it was finished but never released, because in the end Firestone disliked it and refused to grant permission for it to be screened.

Thirty years later, the filmmaker Elisabeth Subrin would make an extraordinary frame-by-frame recreation of this archival film with the actress Kim Soss playing

Shulie. She did this against Firestone's wishes, which seemed like a brave and principled gesture, like something the younger Shulamith Firestone herself might have done, because the work had such value. But by then, Firestone had become extremely suspicious, reclusive.

The following year, Firestone's book *Airless Spaces*—which she described as a "series of vignettes" depicting life on the inside of public psychiatric hospitals—was published by Semiotext(e). Shulamith attended the launch of her book that we arranged at a small East Village gallery on Avenue A. She was too shy to read from the book, so the reading was done by some of her friends: among them, the visionary feminist theorist Kate Millett who, like Shulamith, had shuttled in and out of psychiatric institutions. Firestone leaned against the brick wall while her friends read, beaming.

A few months after she finished art school, Firestone moved to New York and into a small East Village apartment on E. 2nd Street. A few years later, she found a second apartment on E. 10th Street where she'd live for the rest of her life. The place was on East Tenth Street between First and Second Avenues—"the other side of the tracks," as she describes it in one of these stories, casually but very precisely parsing the difference between the quality of life in the neighborhoods east and west of Second Avenue.

She does this over and over again. The very short stories in *Airless Spaces* masterfully depict all kinds of minor atrocities that eventually lead to each person's downfall: a forced shower, a snub, a slow-moving bureaucracy, a repurposed lounge. The facts themselves are the commentary. As in Pialat's *Naked Childhood* or Bresson's *Au hasard Balthazar*, all of the characters in *Airless Spaces* are set on a slow but inevitable downward trajectory. Firestone's goal as a writer is to show us exactly how they got there. The book contains a section called "Losers" but no antonymic section called "Winners," because who ever wins, really? It's no coincidence that Firestone read a great deal of Dostoevsky.

The stories in *Airless Spaces* all demonstrate the confluence between the relatively smooth movement of institutional control and the erratic and sludgy course of the lives of its subjects. The institution's systemic actions are almost always the catalyst for the small tragedies that occur in each of these stories. But as Firestone shows, the system's casual brutality has a powerful afterlife. Over and over, we see the resulting psychic disintegration attain a life of its own, finally enmeshing the subject in paralyzed entropy.

As a very young woman Shulamith Firestone attended civil rights and antiwar demonstrations. She briefly considered aligning herself with the Catholic Marxist organization the Catholic Worker. But by the time she left Chicago, Firestone was already disillusioned with the New Left and its marginalization of women's concerns. In New York, she cofounded a group called New York Radical Women, where female activists from different leftist organizations met to discuss their concerns. As Susan Faludi writes in her beautiful essay on Firestone's life, "Death of a Revolutionary," Radical Women was the first New York group of its kind: a place where women got together to talk about their lives, a place where political principles crystallized through the sharing of each person's experience. She was radicalized further when she and her feminist colleagues at a New Left demonstration were heckled and booed off the stage. In 1969 Firestone organized the first abortion speak-out at Judson Memorial Church in New York. She was directly or indirectly involved in dozens of radical-feminist actions and groups. At the same time—at age twenty-four and in just a few months—she wrote *The Dialectic of Sex*, which became a feminist and radical-activist classic.

Subtitled *The Case for Feminist Revolution*, *The Dialectic of Sex* called upon readers to conduct an analysis of the "sex war" as comprehensive as Marx and Engels's analysis of the class struggle that occurs within dialectical materialism. In fact, such an analysis would be "more comprehensive," she wrote. "For we are dealing ... with an oppression that goes back beyond recorded history to the animal kingdom. ... Feminists have to question, not just all of *Western* culture, but the organization of culture itself." *Dialectic* also famously proposed Firestone's "'dream' action"—a smile boycott where "all women would instantly abandon their 'pleasing' smiles, henceforth smiling only when something pleased *them*."

Shulamith believed the revolution would start when women stopped smiling.

The Dialectic of Sex was released as a mass-market paperback and published in multiple languages. Thousands of women read *The Dialectic of Sex* when it came out and felt like their lives had been changed by it. The book had that power, analysis coupled with rage. I read it when I was fifteen and could not stop observing the traitorous smiles of my classmates and teachers and friends. Firestone wrote presciently about technology, gender, and childhood, and the book remains a powerful influence.

Like Kate Millett's *Sexual Politics* and Germaine Greer's The *Female Eunuch, The Dialectic of Sex* became a very popular book and Shulamith was invited to present the feminist case on network TV. Despite her extreme disdain for celebrity media culture, she became a respected and recognized public figure. And this turned out to be a grave problem within the New York feminist-cadre circles that she led and belonged to.

By the time *Dialectic* was published in 1970, American radical feminism was already moving toward a New Agey essentialism of moon-goddess rites and "total democracy" that seemed to borrow a page from Maoist China's cultural revolution. Leadership and all forms of distinction came to be deeply resented. Those who asserted themselves as speakers were publicly criticized and then finally denounced. Firestone—who refused to "democratically" share in office-housekeeping tasks of her cadre—was accused of "hoarding attention" and being "too intellectual." She was formally censured and then expelled from more than one of the groups that she had founded.

Firestone touches on this devastation very lightly in the story "Myrna Glickman" in the "Obits" section of *Airless Spaces*. Her avatar Rozzie comes back into touch with her former best friend Myrna Glickman through a mutual friend after more than two decades. Myrna, she explains, had once collaborated with Rozzie's powerful enemy Leslie Modrell to oust her from their "supposedly leaderless" feminist group so that Leslie could assume control and eventually run it into the ground. But these struggles are now far in the past. The crux of the story concerns Myrna's less-than-spectacular life after her life as an activist—she and Leslie now meet once a week to play poker together—and how her strange turns of behavior are abruptly explained by a diagnosis of terminal brain cancer.

Firestone didn't publish any more books until *Airless Spaces* came out in 1998. What did she do during those decades? She was not diagnosed schizophrenic or hospitalized until 1987, but there must have been problems before that. By the time the neighbors complained that she screamed through the night and her sister Laya flew into New York to take care of her, Shulamith was completely emaciated, convinced that her food contained poison, and in the street begging.

During the next five years she cycled in and out of public psychiatric facilities regularly—never voluntarily, always on forcible hold. She came to know the language and logic of institutional life intimately: the "activities" and "treats," the "group walk" and "community," all connoted with quotes in these stories.

In the early 1990s, several women—medical staff, a few younger artists and writers who all recognized Shulamith Firestone's tremendous influence and importance—gathered around her as a kind of support group. For a few years, this helped her to stabilize, and it was during these years that she wrote these stories.

Sometime in 1997 Beth Stryker, who was one of Shulamith's younger friends, sent us the manuscript. Would Semiotext(e) like to publish Shulamith Firestone's new, second book? I think we said yes right away before even reading it. But when we finally did, I was just blown away by the way that *Airless Spaces* wasn't a memoir. It wasn't a story of her mental illness and it wasn't driven by any attempt to reconcile or explain her descent into psychosis. Rather, it was as if she'd embedded herself to bear witness to the secret, banal workings of the institution.

Still, as Shulamith notes wryly in her story "Stabilized, Yes," to be stable isn't the same thing as to be happy, or even content. Sometime after the publication of *Airless Spaces* she relapsed, and in August 2012 she died in her apartment.

Shulamith Firestone grew up in St. Louis, Missouri, one of six siblings in an Orthodox Jewish family. From her earliest youth she rebelled against them and their religion bitterly. Still, rereading these stories, I'm struck by how

Jewish they are on both a secular and spiritual level. Ranging in length between a single paragraph and several pages, Firestone's stories are a lot like Talmudic *mashals*—exemplary stories or parables that allegorically demonstrate deeper truths or ideas.

At the same time, it's the way that Firestone chooses to focus on people's very modest ambitions and goals—release from the hospital before Christmas, finding a dark, quiet place to sleep in during the day, controlling the thermostat—that breaks your heart over and over. Often, Firestone's people become the most powerful instruments of their own unhappiness. Eighty-two-year-old Pauline tortures herself over the selection of classical music in "Radio Station WISS." And in "The Caregivers," Berenice, short of money, becomes her neighbor Cleo's part-time caregiver, simultaneously pitying her new client and deeply resenting her.

There are rules to observe if you want to get out of the hospital, as these stories demonstrate: shutting up, signing up for "activities," repressing your "negativity," kissing ass, earnestly composing answers to the empty, absurd prompts on their questionnaires, and all in all, allowing the institution to break you.

To Firestone, the hospital is a microcosm of the larger world. Everything moves through channels of power.

Airless Spaces

For Lourdes Cintron
—as promised in the hospital—

I dreamed I was on a sinking ship. It was a luxury liner like the *Titanic*. The water was slowly seeping up from below, and the people aboard the ship knew that they were doomed. On the two top decks it was gaiety and mirth, with people dressed to the nines, eat drink and be merry for soon we shall all die. But a note of hysteria hovered in the merrymaking and here and there I saw strange goings-on, like in a Grosz cartoon.

I fled down some metal stairs to where people were starting to get their pants legs wet. Wasn't I looking in the wrong direction? But I desperately searched the equipment in the basement for something that would supply an air pocket, and I succeeded in finding a refrigerator into which I stowed myself, hoping to live on even after the boat was fully submerged until it should be found.

I woke from this dream in a panic that this disaster was real, and that I was picking all this up by ESP. I even called UPI to ask if there was any recent news of a sinking liner, and they said yes, but it was in the Bermuda Triangle, so no attempt would be made to find the ship.

OF PLASTIC WRAPPING AND CAULIFLOWER

As soon as she came out of the institution, she tried to put into effect her resolution to eat only fresh fruits and vegetables. She had gained fifty pounds and looked terrible. She was tired of the constant fight to tear open plastic utensils and napkins and small packets of salt and sugar with her bare and palsied hands. She longed for real silverware, especially knives, and to that end she went out and got a vegetable cleaver in Chinatown and a good serrated bread knife.

One night she was going to dine on cauliflower when she was defeated by that damned plastic wrapping again. It was rolled on very tight and neither of her knives knew what to do. She finally decided to chop through the roll, only to take off a piece of her little finger with it, causing much blood and pain, and a visit to the emergency room of St. Vincent's.

A home nutritionist was sent out, a Creole, who decided this old lady was no longer able to cook for herself. She was enrolled in a meals-on-wheels program and so came back to cursing the mashed potato whip and the insulated plastic dining utensils, not to mention the sugar and salt.

HOSPITAL

THE FORCED SHOWER

Corinne was waiting for the Environmental Control Board to send in a water-inspection team. In fact, she knew they had already been in the hospital, and the word was to bring those water levels up to normal. In the meantime, she had been without a shower so long a few more days would hardly make any difference. The thing is, you see, she actually wanted a shower, just not one with 40 percent formaldehyde in it. She had waited many months because the water in her apartment had 116 different poisons in it, all listed in the CIA manual, which is how you knew they were hard poisons and not just the "medication" that was pretended. She narrowly escaped seizure at mealtime by double-guessing them and hastily rinsing under her arms, though she was sure she had long since stopped sweating. Still, one of the aides nosed into her room and said, "Get ready for your shower, girl, one way or the other." It was about eight thirty at night and shower times were usually in the mornings. She guessed they had missed her at dinner. Now she willed them with all her strength to go away and forget about her. She was genuinely surprised when this didn't work. The whole team appeared at her door about fifteen minutes after the warning, security cops and all. She went limp. Someone took each of her four limbs and someone else cradled her head. "But I agreed to take a shower as soon as the water levels pass inspection," she protested to no one in particular. Her limp body practically brushed the floor, only the stiff limbs held up.

They took her to one of the showers off the private rooms, the one which was inhabited by the ancient Chinese crone who needed a twenty-four-hour attendant. A stool filled most of the small shower. They forced her down on this even though she was still going limp for the cameras, so much so that her torso hung limp from the waist all the way to the floor, her arms flapping. Then they got brutal, all with merriment. (She had always noticed that the more security cops were on the job, the more of a good time they all had. Maybe they were posing for some candid camera too.) One soaped between her legs and another got her hair worked into a stiff lather. She was beyond yelling that the soap was worse than the water, being about 89 percent chemicals. How did she know all this? It was simple. Read the label of the shampoo body wash. Didn't a hospital the size of Beth Abraham have even some leftover Ivory soap from ten years ago? Was the budget so weak you had to wash with what amounted to a glorified paper towel full of medication and pure chemicals?

"She's anorexic too. She hasn't been eating, she's lost even more weight since she got in here."

"How would you know? You've never even seen me undressed before or taken my weight," Corinne shot back. They had her standing naked up against the small mob of attendants crowded into the bathroom.

"Evelyn Eldred," Corinne read her name off her badge, actually jabbing her with her index finger in the throat area, "you are fired!" Evelyn's face contorted, and she pulled out of her pocket a couple of needles. "Hold her down," she said, and with maximum impact they jabbed her in each naked buttock as she stood there leaning up against them.

"You forgot to wash the soap out of my hair" was her last attempt before they dragged her out limp again and dumped her on her bed. Someone grabbed her long tangled soapy hair and pulled it to the top of her head on the side under a rubber band. The lights were glaring and she managed through the sedative from the shot to ask someone to turn off the light. "Turn it off yourself," said a big Black woman, one of the guards.

Corinne lay there for hours in a daze. Not exactly the shower she had dreamt of. She doubted she was even clean. But that she would have to conquer her fears and take showers herself from now on there could be no doubt. She wasn't going to let herself be put through this again. She didn't think she could stand it. And why did they sedate her at the end when it was all over rather than at first? Because she dared to wave a finger at the head aide. They treated you as a leper, they were scared of patient aggression, the smallest infraction brought out the whole battery.

Corinne went to mealtimes like a wounded creature for some days. Her dreadlock served only to remind the staff of what she had just been through. It was matted and stiff with chemicals but she had already tried to get a brush with no luck. All she had was a semibrush for pocket or purse, so it was this or nothing. It took hours to comb it out strand by strand and in some places it was so clumped she feared she would just have to cut into it and leave a gaping hole.

Finally, very proud of herself, she managed a modest braid, but she noted that her hair was no longer thick and luxurious but thin and wispy as if the chemicals had burned away whole strands. From here dates Corinne's haircut, which turned out to be a bowl-on-the-head sort of job, what with the exigencies of hospital passes, the money required, and other problems. From this time on Corinne began to look like a mental patient, not an attractive woman who just happened to be thrown into a mental hospital.

THE PRAYER CONTEST

She had exhausted the Om Mane Padme Oms and Hare Krishna Rama Krishnas and was on to calling the angels Gabriel and Raphael when they switched her into a back room on the other side of the square. Ms. Poland, as Leora called her because she couldn't master her name, sniffed like a cat claiming her turf, and indicated she could not have the window bed. Ms. Poland was a broad fat blond over fifty, or she looked that way due to her Central European origin, where presumably there was nothing to retard the aging process. Immigration problems are all that's wrong with her, Leora decided.

She had a husband too, who was every inch a husband, right down to the conjugal visits with kielbasa and soda, and sharing the bathroom. In between Ms. Poland did exercises, masturbated against her broad right arm, and moaned, with or without the masturbation. She also cried tenderly from time to time. Leora was hard put to continue her chanting with this whole show going on.

Finally she just did it anyway. Ms. Poland, not to be outdone, began in a warbling voice to sing the Polish national anthem, and threw in a few Russian national favorites too. Leora held her ground and continued to chant for her favorite angels. Exasperated, Ms. Poland now began Kyrie Eleison and what she remembered of the mass, and threw in a few rosaries to Mary as well. Leora figured she had better shut up.

BEDTIME IS THE BEST TIME OF DAY

When Holly was brought into the hospital on involuntary all she wanted to do was crash, that is, sleep all day and night to escape her imprisonment. While this lasted for many weeks as a good solution, the day came when her body could hibernate no more. Sleeping no longer felt good. But still there was nothing to get up for, and moreover she was in a permanent state of drowse.

She tried to train herself not to sleep during the day, because the absolute worst was to get trapped at lights out all raring to go. It was hard. There was little to do, and nowhere to go on a shut-in psychiatric ward but her bed. At home when she had missed a night of sleep, she had slept all day, been up again till the wee hours when at last she had allowed herself to sleep till noon; but then it got later and later, 3:00 p.m., 5:00 p.m., until some lucky day when she was able to sleep around the clock and wake up at nine to start a fresh sleep cycle. And failing that, to brave it out for twenty-four hours without any sleep at all or until she was so dead she could just fall into bed.

Here in the hospital there was no such freedom of hours. You were woken at seven and then frequent meal-times and then constant interruptions and scheduled "activities" for which you had to leave your room or be checked off as sick. The trouble was, now that her hibernation cycle was used up temporarily, she could not drop off to sleep at a moment's notice, to sleep for, say, an hour that happened to be free, because for that she had to be hungry for sleep and she was, instead, oversatiated. She found it increasingly impossible to sleep during the day, so afraid she was of not being tired at lights-out time. But even with a sleeping pill she could not sleep at night either. And she was worried about the sleeping pills, because Ativan was as addictive as Valium, and she didn't want to leave the hospital with a habit, one moreover which required a prescription.

This is how she ended up an insomniac on the waiting list for the Sleep Disorder wing of the psychiatric hospital.

DEBRA DAUGHERTY

Around the big square seating arena that made up the communal room, used for doctor interviews, patient visits, and just lounging, Queenie reigned from a corner almost-booth where the magazines were stacked (when there were any). She was a mulatto anorexic with depression and crying jags, but she was at the end of her stay at Beth Abraham, and so she literally beamed warmth and good cheer. She curled up in her Queenie's seat at the head of the square and from there kept up quite a lively social life as bottom woman to all the drifter men around, and quite a few women she was friendly with too. The question was, when she left, who would replace her, since there was no woman near her in seniority, and quite simply, no woman together enough on the ward at the time to stand in for her. She ordered her meals carefully and ate daintily, with obvious relish, so that even if you wanted to puke at your own meal, she made you jealous of her food (which was after all only the same old hospital food that you got).

She swung her hair, which may have been a wig, she bothered with makeup, especially when going out on a pass, and she kept all the male interest vying but in its place in the small circle around her at mealtimes. Shades of Nefertiti, she ate so much but still remained thin, graceful and erect. (She must have been skinny as a noodle when she came in.) All the men prepared to miss her as talk of her discharge date became more frequent.

For a week or even two after she left, nobody dared to sit in Queenie's former seat at the head of the square couch. Then one day there were a couple of new admissions; both looked to be in bad shape. One was Arthur, a Black man, very small and delicate and intense, who spoke like someone in a halfway house bursting with plans, and with some grandiosity about his philosophies. I could only think that a few days in Beth Abraham would knock the shit out of him and I was right. The rules and regulations proved too much for him and in a matter of days he was being wheeled around in a wheelchair, his saliva white and pasty from new medications, trailing a row of cookies he had managed to commandeer at various long-awaited snack times from people who felt sorry for him. (He had announced he wanted to regain the forty pounds he had lost when he was on the street.)

But the other admission who lay out on the couches instead of her assigned bed for sheer restlessness was a woman, named Debra Daugherty, an obviously once-beautiful chick who now looked like a wasted Appalachian from a Dorothea Lange photography show of the thirties. In other words, "white trash." Her teeth were bad and her posture hung. Her eyes were a lusterless green. Her hair was lank and dank. But she innocently took up Queenie's old space, where she would lie, limbs akimbo, most of the night and day, complaining incessantly in a rather raucous voice about how life had done her in. This was no Queenie in command, but a poor wretch that everyone navigated to get around—unless she was on the phone blocking the hallway, explaining her case yet again.

But they didn't let you sleep out on the sofas for long. That was just for new admissions who hadn't gotten the hang of the place yet, who hadn't yet found the track to discharge. And it's true that it took Debra an unusually long time to figure out the game. There she stood in her hospital robes pleading her case on the phone, or collapsed into a heap on the public sofas, ignoring everyone, until finally she was put in a dormitory room where it was made clear she had to sleep every night.

I began to try to cue her in: "If you want to get out of here, Dr. Barnes is the chief honcho, you're wasting your time on Costa," "You have to attend all the 'activities' religiously," and so forth. She proved impervious to all such advice at first, but still made her presence felt with the most surprising audacity in demanding clothes from the hospital staff on grounds that someone she had last been sleeping with had thrown out her bedding and her clothing without a thought. She actually achieved an all-white hospital jumpsuit and one used baggy purple sweater which, however, became her; and other clothes followed. Since it did matter how soon one began to "dress," Debra surprised me by suddenly becoming more visible on the ward and therefore more likely to be put on the fast track out.

Because she did not yet have the status for "passes" to leave the hospital, I found myself, on "group walk," remembering to save her a couple of cigarettes or some candy orange slices—how she could smoke the cigarettes in a no-smoke hospital, however, was not an easy one to solve, especially as she had finally started showing an active interest in working her way out of the place and didn't want to attract a bad scene. She showed some interest in a cooking class and was a natural at crafts, and so she soon attracted the attention of the "OT" (occupational therapist in charge of patient "activities"). So it seemed she had her own instinctive way out of the place, and really didn't need my advice, which had worked for me, anyway. At any rate, my good news that I would be out before Christmas was soon followed by her own cautious optimism that she might get out the week after I did, which is to say Christmas Eve proper.

Lots of others talked it, but did not move; but Debra and I got out. I surprised myself by missing her enough to call her at the hospital (usually I forgot the hospital and everybody in it just as soon as I could) and promised her some old clothes and before long I had taken down her address and promised to visit after Christmas.

I found her on Avenue D in a strange newly constructed housing situation: all the apartments were small and hotelish and you couldn't go up past the man in the cage (I hesitate to say doorman) unless personally escorted on the elevator by the person whose guest you were. She had told me on the phone of her embarrassment that she had left her place "trashed," and that about described it: mounds of dirty clothes covered the floor and bare bed, old ashtrays, dirty dishes in the sink, but I could see even through this that it was a cute little unit with a good bathroom, though only one blindered window. She had disability and the building was Section 8 which meant she got a certain discount in the rent and was paying only $179 or so. There was even a community room with a good cable TV and if you opened a certain cabinet, computer access to email—though I saw no one other than a couple of old men in there at any time.

I went there with a couple of too-small wool sweaters but they were too small on her too; but I came back with a green cotton sweater which had some heavy creases in the wrong places, which I thought I might disguise with a scarf. I watched her attack the mound around her bed— she apologized for killing a cockroach on the wall with her bare hand—and bring down the laundry to the community washing machine. She said my company helped and I was pleased. She was terrified someone in authority would see the way the room was trashed and send her back to the hospital. That first visit was just before Christmas and she was agitated about going home (Throgs Neck, the Bronx) so unprepared. She had a son and in-laws in that neighborhood, though her own parents were recently dead. She talked endlessly about her husband, how he had tried to kill her on their honeymoon, how he had ruined her life and made her "sick," how she had to win over their son, and on and on. That first time we ate in a little Spanish dive right near her house, practically the only place open for a long stretch in that bombed-out neighborhood. I remember how afraid she was to go into stores she had been thrown out of and couldn't even remember it. She said she had a girlfriend whom she might meet for a New Year's Eve drink—did I mention her drinking problem??—and she said I should come along too.

I talked to Debra on the phone in the interim, and it seemed Christmas had gone well enough. (I never knew how she pulled it together to get out there that day; I myself was always only barely functional after the hospital, where I was heavily medicated, made few decisions, and slept around the clock.) Her family had given her a set of Clinique cosmetics, which was better than their usual bad-taste gifts. But again she went over the same stories about her husband almost killing her on her honeymoon, and all that, until I began to feel I shouldn't be seeing someone in her condition on the first night of the year. But she said she was bringing her friend, "you would really like her," so I repressed my doubts. What could go wrong with a harmless drink at the Life Cafe on Tenth Street, meeting someone

I had known at the hospital and a possibly interesting friend of hers?

I arrived at her place spruced up for a little bar hopping and I saw that she was too. But her "friend" was a no-show and she immediately began to berate her as the most selfish girl in the world. I soon noticed she was sloppy drunk. Sitting alone in the community room waiting for me, she had been through a six-pack. I attempted to hide my disappointment and go through with it. I had made no other plans.

We went to the café and she ordered a vodka gimlet. When she ordered the second one, I reminded her I wouldn't be able to walk her home, as I lived in the other direction. She narrowed her eyes, took a deep drag on her cigarette, and said, "You're getting judgmental, aren't you?"

"I suppose so, but I don't think you should have any more. Why don't you try some food?"

"Because I haven't eaten in two days and I have a stomach virus. And why don't you try going home now instead of later?"

"I think I will," I said, reaching for my jacket.

Should I have felt guilty leaving her like that to get ploughed under? I didn't feel like feeling guilty; I was only afraid I had caught her stomach flu. Oh well, there might still be time to get back and watch the ball fall in Times Square on TV, if I hurried.

BLOODWORK

At eight in the morning, in the cold rain, Roberta made her way to Beth Abraham for a routine blood test. Was it lab requirements that made blood tests always in the gray early morning, on an empty stomach? She was out of the hospital now, but not so long ago they had been testing her as an in-patient for Tegretol reactions: thirteen blood tests in a row, until the glaring lights-on orderlies with their trays, hunting through the rows of comatose bodies for her name, became all mixed up with her morning awakening. Although she too hoped for a "nice" orderly, she was full of contempt for some of her roommates who obsequiously thanked the orderlies for the little operation when they were through. Her elbow veins were always difficult, beginning with a syphilis test once in a VD clinic in which the sadistic doctor had gotten blood smeared all over her arm, trying to stem the flow with rough brown paper towels. Now she like as not circumnavigated the whole mess by clenching her thumb and forefinger and extending the mound it made to the orderly for penetration. The trick was never to look.

"Imagine it's a mosquito bite," said one Spanish attendant, trying to be helpful. Some mosquito bite! Roberta swore she would never get used to it.

THE TURKISH FILMMAKER

He stood out on the ward immediately. Wild, handsome, though with bad skin and the beginning of the paunch of middle age, this character did not belong in a ward full of adolescents and old ladies. One wondered how he would find his way out, and what brought him in in the first place.

I was attracted to him, I can tell you that. I surveyed my lost figure and my once-gorgeous hair and knew I looked blah now. But still I thought if I could make myself useful he would be a friend to me. I found out he was a Turkish filmmaker who had tried to put himself out via carbon monoxide from the stove. He had grants at City College and some other places to do educational specials.

My chance to speak to him came. Once he was sentenced to an indeterminate stay in the ward I tried to come to his aid with helpful information. "The only way to get out fast is to have people on the outside rooting for you. Have someone call about you repeatedly and say you are needed for a film shoot and time lost is money lost."

It appeared he had a girlfriend who was a partner who could do this admirably. "Thank you. Now what do I do while I'm in here to kill time?"

I shared my big secret. "You pace."

"You mean you walk around? There's nowhere to walk."

"That's why you have to do it systematically. You cover the corridors back and forth even when they're busy. You might even try counting. Or doing it with a companion."

He considered this as if I were loco, but in the next few days, as I knew it would, his boredom became so painful that he would try anything. Unfortunately for me, it was not me he chose as his pacing partner, but rather a beautiful Chinese girl whom I particularly disliked. She was a goody-good who did not seem to have any mental problem at all, just homelessness. Together they walked the halls, chatting it up, and they made it look almost normal except that they were always there. Meanwhile, my advice to keep up the outside pressure was also working and wheels were turning. I saw his girlfriend come to visit him: she was a tall, heavy, striking actress in a cape. As for patient "activities," which everyone had to prove himself in before any kind of discharge, I was surprised to see him flattering the young therapists and getting around them that way. Just counting the days till his discharge.

I tried once more before he left. I had left my checkbook in my apartment which was near where he lived. They wouldn't let me leave the ward under any circumstances since I was "involuntary" and would probably never come back. I didn't have a friend I was speaking to and I had no way to pay my rent.

One morning at six o'clock I was tormented with the idea that I should go to him and ask him to go to my apartment. The urgency of it told me that it was more than my rent worry involved, that I was afraid I would never see him again.

I snuck into his room and stood there for some time watching his sleeping back. He looked large and heavy, a husband figure. I could just imagine waking up to that sleeping bulk day after day.

Well, the upshot was I didn't have the nerve to ask him for this favor. I did see him again, once on the street in passing, when he barely said hello; and once at a Westbeth opening, where he was with a striking girl, the same or another one, and he didn't say hello. But I distinctly saw him give his phone number to the Chinese girl with whom he had paced the halls according to my best advice.

THERMOSTAT CONTROL

Bettina had severe insomnia and the loveless hospital only made it worse. Her nerves were worn to rag ends from long months without even a blink or two—she heard that was impossible but she could swear to it—and getting through the trying day in the dormitory became progressively harder without that buffer which is sleep. Sometimes she hardly remembered what she craved; but once when she actually fell asleep for about fifteen minutes toward dawn, she woke feeling like a queen: "Who am I? Where am I?" It seems she'd even been having a dream or was on the edges of one. But try as she might she could not bring back this form of blissful escape. She took her Ativan at night, hoping every night, but though she felt a slight pull, a kind of nip and tuck, she didn't go under. She was wired. And what's more she couldn't even get comfortable in the hospital bed. She was used to a big double bed on the floor, without springs, the kind you sink into; and the high narrow hospital cot, with the overstuffed polyester pillow, kept her rigid all night. Then there was the restlessness that came from the Haldol she was on, a very high dose. Her spine hurt and she wanted to jump out of her skin. In the night's wee hours, that is right before the blood test teams came in and the morning shift changed, somewhere in the hour of the wolf, she took to circling around her bed and counting. She couldn't go out in the hall more than once a night without being written down for sleeplessness, which would lower her status toward getting out. But even in this she had to be careful, for fear of the fifteen-minute head counts all night long. She began circling her bed when they left and jumped back in bed according to her watch when the next head count was due.

Then one day someone complained about the warm temperature in the room, and a nurse was sent in to lower it. Bettina had never noticed the little wheel on the wall because only the short metal rod showed, wherever it had been "set"—but the wheel itself was firmly locked behind the counter of the nursing station. Now she indeed noticed the change in the temperature: there was an icebox chill to the air all night which Bettina took a perverse pleasure in. "If I can't sleep, at least I can chill out," she giggled to herself. And she began to concentrate on lying absolutely still as a corpse. This gave relief somehow; it was better than pacing around her bed, and, while not exactly refreshing, it simulated sleep somewhat.

In the morning there were complaints about the coldness of the room, but most people were unaware of the wheel or what to do about it. Meanwhile Bettina looked forward to bedtime with a new eagerness.

After some days, personnel was summoned again, but there were so many arguments about which temperature the wheel should be turned to that in the end it was left in the room. Bettina was aghast that her new substitute for sleep was about to be pulled out from under her. She appointed herself controller of the thermostat and took the wheel right off the wall and put it in her robe pocket. No one would ever know the difference.

It took some days for the complaints to build up again, and for personnel to notice that the wheel was missing. "I have a bad cold, and I know what's causing it," said Ms. Lee, an old enemy of Bettina since their scuffle over the opening or closing of the hospital curtains during the night. (Bettina wanted them open so she could see the dawn breaking as she counted the grueling hours till seven o'clock wake-up.)

Bettina considered and knew her time was up. Soon there would be a hunt for the thermostat control dial and direct suspicions would be brought to bear. She put it back on the wall. It wasn't long before it was spotted and the temperature was shot up to accommodate the increasing complaints of her roommates.

Bettina was miserable again in her bed and back to pacing around it in the hour of the wolf, with no sleep in sight. A sentinel like the Green Giant stood guard over her body to make sure that she didn't dose off even once the whole night long.

SWOONING

After they raised her dose to 42 mg of Trilafon, Lucy very nearly fainted. She felt a rush of bad sensation comparable to her mental telepathy when her grandmother died (that lasted about three days) in which all the blood rushed to her head and when it rushed back again she felt old and ready to die.

But there was a good aspect to fainting too. As she was about to lose consciousness she felt an overwhelming relief. The black-velvety edges of the swoon. If only she could faint all the way, blackout, and never wake up again.

THINKING NEGATIVE

This new old lady that had just entered Beth Abraham definitely spooked Phyllis. Her name was Helen, and she was small and gray and moustached, a reject. She was on the phone all day to her sister, giving her virtually hourly reports of her progress, probably unsolicited, and she was alarmingly candid. "But I don't know what to do with myself all day," she would loudly complain, "between breakfast and lunch, between lunch and dinner, between dinner and 8:30 p.m. snack. I can't do 'activities,'" she would protest, "they're ridiculous. Why should I wave an umbrella parachute up and down with five other women?" she would ask querulously. "What do I need a mosaic coffee stand for, unless I get out? And that reminds me, when am I getting out? I thought I could just sign myself out if it didn't work out. Why can't I? If you'll just listen, I'm telling you why it's not working out. It's the boredom all day and at night too. You know there's nothing to read here. You know the papers are a day old and all missing.

At least at home I can read the papers all morning over my coffee, I can take a walk," and so on.

One day a walk was scheduled outside the hospital, with coffee stopover. Helen kept complaining like a drizzle. The escort, a German social worker with a merry round face full of compassion, kept saying, Helen, why are you so negative? You find nothing but fault, look at the bright side, you're going for an outing with friends and the coffee is free. Helen resisted this: I thought I could sign myself out if it didn't work out, why can't I? and so forth. The social worker merely humored her patiently, to everybody's annoyance (they all wanted to tell her to shut up, she was ruining their little trip out), without responding directly to her queries.

Phyllis was aghast: There but for the grace of God indeed. In what way was she different from Helen other than a few years younger? She too had a sister whom she called, her closest family connection. Would her sister one day get tired of the "negativity" and just leave her inside for good, the phone calls gradually easing off?

THE OLD FOLKS' HOME

Karen told the group about her ninety-seven-year-old grandmother who, after her husband died, had tried to kill herself three times with sleeping pills, but they had her stomach pumped. She was watched carefully at mealtimes, when a guard would bark at her to eat. Don't ever end up in a place like this, she warned her granddaughter. And she shed tears at the unaccustomed tenderness of gesture when Karen tucked in her old light-blue comforter up around her chin as she sat in her wheelchair.

ELLIN RUBIE

Ellin Rubie popped up in my ward one day, assuring me she remembered me from school, though I couldn't exactly recall her. She had a toothy grin and red hair and, in a hospital context, she looked more like a visitor than a patient. She was youthful, cheerful, and didn't seem sick.

I had only a few more days to go on the ward, but in that time I heard her story: She had been reared in Waukegan, Illinois, went to college in Ann Arbor— University of Michigan—and had somehow made it to Yale for postgraduate work in art and design. She had taught at Amherst for a number of years, long enough to save money to buy a whole building in the Flower District (the West Twenties and Thirties in Manhattan). She lived in her own loft, though the lofts in her building were commercially restricted to work hours only.

She had "gotten sick" but no one believed there was anything wrong with her. Even the doctors thought she was a hypochondriac. She had been through every medication in the book (and indeed, I ended up borrowing her beaten-up old manual, scored with notes), and even diagnoses related to congenital epilepsy didn't seem to help. Now she was in the hospital for electroconvulsive therapy, which she assured me was not as horrific as it used to be. She looked forward to it almost eagerly, and I remember seeing her one day in the elevator being taken by the orderlies down to the EKG room sitting primly in a wheelchair with a brave smile on her face. By the time she finished with this series of about thirteen or so treatments I was out of the hospital, but I called to find out how it had gone: inconclusive, as always.

In the years that followed, I made a point of maintaining contact with Ellin: I wanted to have at least one new friend that was halfway normal from my hospital ordeal. I found out she was gay, and the young man who visited her was her paid aide, not her boyfriend or husband. She had a girlfriend of long standing, but this affair was breaking up due to her protracted illness. She also had a strong tie to a female doctor of some standing, head of In-Psychiatry for the large hospital. She was always going for hospital stays of weeks or months and then was unreachable. I visited her in one of these with some flowers: she was literally "wired": there was a big clump of wires attached to the back of her head and trailing her bare feet when she got out of bed to go to the bathroom. But she was cheerful through it all, and observed herself objectively, as a psychiatrist would. Then there was a long stay at Johns Hopkins in Baltimore for more tests and experimentation. After she got through this, and came back to town, I met her for dinner and found that she was really distraught. She had trusted her brother to manage her property, and now he was suing for ownership on grounds that she was mentally ill and couldn't manage it.

She was furious at this lie, and I could see why. I knew she was one of the few mental patients who was quite competent. I did not understand her art (I hoped that *she* did), but she seemed quite a competent concierge of her building, and I was impressed that she kept down her weight under heavy-duty medication by swimming at the nearby Y sometimes several times a day. She showed other indications of a strong self-discipline, and she was not soft and lazy, as one sometimes gets in the hospital, but energetic and with plenty of initiative.

In any case, she was determined to fight her brother's aggression, and to pay any amount necessary to keep her property. She hired a big-time lawyer for the mentally ill and sued her brother in reverse for breach of contract. Every time I talked to her on the phone after that she was overloaded by the litigation and to be even halfway sociable she had to will herself not to discuss the case. When I met her for dinner I began to notice her costume was zany, her red hair thinning (she said too much Depakote was making it curl) and her red lipstick smeared. She was distressed and obsessed with the litigation, the unspoken subject of all meetings. She couldn't simply relax and have fun.

Then I didn't call her for a long time. I intended to invite her to come to my therapy group, but had second thoughts about it, since I feared she might do a sales pitch for various medications she was enthusiastic about. She was on about eight medications at once, in small doses. Whereas I myself was usually leery of medication.

When finally I called, I got the operator in a recording: *The number you have reached has been disconnected. No further information is available.* Evidently the worst had happened. Her brother had won the lawsuit, and not content with owning the property long distance, had demanded her ouster as a tenant, even though she told me that she had been willing to negotiate a division of floors. She had spent her last cent on lawyers, and would have been left penniless.

There was no way to reach her, and she was not in the habit of calling me.

I took her name off my Rolodex.

THE JUMPSUIT

Ana came into the hospital by police force in the dog days of August and they neglected to bring any of her clothes with her. She wrote a refusal to see all visitors, and had none anyhow, since she didn't call anyone to let them know her whereabouts. She got by on the cheap toothbrushes and small tubes of Everest hospital toothpaste and by remaining in hospital pajamas for longer than required. By mid-November, even in the thermostat-controlled environment, without drafts from any windows (all the windows were permanently sealed), she was still refusing to cooperate with nurses' aides unless they brought her a warm sweatshirt, a pair of socks (she was still wearing the sandals she came in with as all-purpose shoes, slippers, and even quite nakedly as shower clogs), and a hair brush (she had been getting by on a pocket comb too thin for her thick tresses). One of them brought her a pair of Kelly-green anklets with an ugly design on the bottom, but these were dirty in three days and she found it difficult to arrange to wash them.

Finally she overheard one of the patients nagging and appealing to Gerald for a jogging suit. Gerald was one of the few good orderlies who actually kept his word and did things for you like unlocking the shower at night. He said he would see what he could do, and this meant (from him only) a certain yes. Ana put in her bid for one too, as appealingly as she could. He was a good man, that Gerald, whom she remembered from previous hospital stays as reliable as clockwork.

When the suits finally came up, they were white and bright. Well, it's better than gray, thought Ana, who felt like a bride wearing it, one of two competing brides. The high visibility of the suit gave her the idea of using it to get on a speed track out of the hospital. She appeared at the Monday morning "community" meeting quite prominently no longer wearing a hospital robe or even the somewhat better but ill-fitting blue pajamas. In her striking new suit she flashed and dazzled the doctors, and she had even combed her hair and stolen some makeup. She did this a few times in a row to build up a record, and then she hit Dr. Tsun, the good foreign one, with a request for a meeting with some previous doctors and nurses familiar with her case in the past.

When she wanted to lose her high profile, she hid away the white suit in her empty drawer and continued to wear the blue pajamas. The rival "bride" had gotten a soup stain on her sweatpants, washed the bottom to gray, and now could no longer wear the sweatshirt and sweatpants together (there was no bleach in the hospital supply room). But Ana saved her wedding dress for important occasions, like her upcoming meeting.

Which she presided over like a queen in haute couture. And she was sprung.

But when she got out of the hospital and tried to wear her dazzling white-sweat outfit in late November, she looked like an escapee from a loony bin rather than a high-fashion model.

Barbara Hoagland was a "voluntary" patient in the hospital for a rest, and that put her way ahead of the other patients, even though by her own standards she was practically dysfunctional. She was a legal secretary—for the past twenty-five years now—and earned well over $50,000 a year, though admittedly with lots of overtime, bonuses, and the rest. She had a nice place in Park Slope, Brooklyn, good friends, and a grown-up daughter.

She was in that menopausal age range, going squat, just about to lose her attractiveness, which was mostly attributable to some good cheek bones and a slightly oriental squint to the eyes, showed off by a good haircut, though she was bleached blond and her roots showed. She brought her own message T-shirts and wore a clean, well-fitting one every day, instead of hospital gowns.

She was soon followed around by a young WASP male investment banker who shared a spacious loft in expensive SoHo with some chic friends and who never left the house with less than sixty dollars in his wallet. He wasn't quite good looking, for though young and thin and blond, he had a crooked nose and a weak chin. He had been raving when brought in, quite in the middle of a psychotic "break." Within days he was on a stiff dose of Haldol, taking baby steps in his stiffness, appealing to other patients as if they were information-desk clerks or sales personnel in a clothing store for information about the place he found himself in. He soon latched onto Barbara. Was it because she was slightly maternal or because you could still imagine how she had looked as a college sophomore—or merely because she was the only unattached WASP female in the ward? Soon he was sitting beside her at mealtimes, which also drew other males and built up her ego with the youthful male attention. But she never lost her head. She knew he was only thirty-two and babyishly spoiled by rich parents—this aside from his psychotic episodes. (When she left all he got was a phone number to help him out in his apartment hunting in her Brooklyn neighborhood—since all his fine-feathered roommates wanted him out because it was his relapse #2.)

You knew she was on the road to recovery when she imparted her mustard-vinaigrette recipe to the cooking class, and her crafts were far and away superior to those working around her. She tended to leaf through crafts magazines brought from home for new ideas for homemade Christmas presents, such as quilts or large wooden angels. No, next to her the other patients looked helpless indeed, and whenever such a patient was found a small circle of energy built up around her.

She was a welcome sight to occupational therapists used to patients who would barely even speak, and was soon going out on "group walk" every day. Soon also she was entertaining visitors, mainly her sophomore daughter (who gave away Barbara's age) and an aging pleasant couple in their sixties who always came bearing flowers or gifts. Instead of turning up her nose at the planned "activities," as many did, Barbara took them seriously. She wrote out carefully considered analyses when asked to fill out questionnaires (of which there were many), such as a simple multiple choice designed to gauge one's consumer habits—whether extravagant or frugal—for a workshop on "Resources." In a workshop on "Self-Esteem" to the question "What is a positive point about yourself or your self-image?" she wrote, "I have sound, strong legs."

YES, WE HAVE NO BANANAS

Like most punks in the hospital, Jane insisted on wearing her own clothes rather than hospital pajamas from the start, but it was mostly her haircut that gave her away as a punk: she wore it short and dyed black and shaved at the neck. She was small and ugly and she wore a lot of makeup under her devil's-eye glasses. She was always sitting on the floor in the hall talking on the phone in a loud voice, trying to get out. It would have been easy to figure out from her conversations just what had been the psychotic episode that had gotten her locked up in the first place, but I didn't bother, I was tuned out. I just wanted her to stop talking so loud.

One morning at seven, the breakfast trays, tagged with names, had small bananas on them, but they forgot to put one on mine. I sat across from Jane, and politely (as is my wont) I asked her if she wanted her banana. She spat in my face, eggs flying, a torrent of incomprehensible abuse following. The breakfast shift came to separate us. It was a big deal.

I thought it would blow over. After all, what had I done but ask for her banana? But she began circulating vicious rumors about me, and so I began to listen in on her phone calls. Gradually I felt that her continual loud slanders and attempts to implicate me—apparently she had been disciplined with a probable setback in status— were working to surround me with malice. I was already an outcast. But I worried that the authorities would use the incident to get me.

Then suddenly she was gone.

POST-HOSPITAL

PATCHED

When she came out of the hospital, her Levi's no longer fit her. She dug through her hand-me-downs to find a pair of scruffy light-blue jeans with big rips at the knees that she had found thrown out in front of an old brownstone. She wore them through the winter with long johns underneath the rip, until at last when spring came, the rip had widened to way beyond fashionable, and it was time to invest in a new pair. Her figure evidently wasn't going to return.

After a confusing and fruitless shopping trip to Canal Jeans, where all three used Levi's were incorrectly sized, and she fled the jammed dressing rooms in despair that she no longer was able to shop, she finally settled on the first pair of jeans about her size she saw in an outdoor rack. They had a hole in exactly the same place as the previous jeans, the right knee, but it was a smaller hole, and since the jeans were a little long she figured unless she wore a belt the tension point of the knee would not fall exactly on the hole and widen it to a rip again. There was a long line waiting for the dressing room, and she didn't have the heart to go through all the jeans in the rack to find the one with a less obtrusive hole, and the very handsome salesboy let her know she couldn't tie up the dressing room any longer even if she wanted to. So she plumped down fifteen bucks, which was the lowest sale price for Levi's anywhere, holes or no holes. Besides, she had already invested two dollars in an iron-on patch from Woolworth's for the old pair, but it was the wrong color for the new pair.

Still stiff from the Haldol she was on, she prevailed upon a friend to help her iron the patch on the new jeans before the hole should widen in the wash. Her little ironing board did not hold up, so they had to use a towel on her butcher-block kitchen table, unplugging the refrigerator to find a near outlet. But after forty-five minutes the patch began to unpeel around the edges and they had to clumsily sew it on, wrong color, oversize, and scrubby, with no guarantee it wouldn't come out in the wash anyway, since she had neglected to sew together the hole before ironing on the patch.

Thus it was that she went from scruffy fashionable with splits at the knees to pickaninny-in-patches wherever she went.

PASSABLE, NOT PRESENTABLE

She remembered the time before she had gotten sick. When it was a challenge to dress, how good it felt to look just right and be certain of one's appearance. Then came losing her looks in the hospital, and the ghastly difference it made in the way she was received; the way people turned away from her after one glance in the street. And the slow climb back, trying to disguise the stiffness in her gait, and the drooling moronic look on her face that came from the medication. Perhaps this was why the mentally disabled always seemed so bland looking as a group: they had to strive to look ordinary, to "pass." That little bit of extra aplomb that made one stand out of the crowd was beyond them.

EMOTIONAL PARALYSIS

Coming out of the hospital, she could not shop. It was more than just the surfeit of goods, which had always confused her. Even a shopping list did not help, she dropped her cart in the middle and fled. Her shelves were lined with missing objects she needed and had almost bought. Even when she succeeded in actually going through with a purchase, she came home dissatisfied with her choice. To pick out a simple birthday card for her more and more distant relatives was agony. She was reminded of those stories of war-torn soldiers who arrived back from years in the army unable to make even the smallest decision. The hospital did that to you: meals were all laid out, but even there she had a hard time choosing any small choices on the menu, and was glad they had dispensed with that pretense and just gave the same thing to everyone every day: a variation on bread and cheese, sometimes a grilled cheese sandwich, sometimes macaroni and cheese; and for dinner it was invariably leg of chicken. She got used to this routine and felt cheated out of her meal if it was anything else. Similarly, just to order deodorant from the gift shop of the hospital was a big deal, and even choosing gum in lieu of the now-banned cigarettes gave her a problem. She had few visitors and they did not as a rule bring her anything she really needed, just clutter for her two or three drawers where she had been wont to squirrel away extra linen. She still didn't have a decent pen or paper.

Her indecision was awful, for no sooner did an impulse arise to do something, than it would be crossed by a contrary impulse; she was conflicted. (She watched herself undergo this in slow motion as it were, but was powerless to avoid it.) Or she was confronted by so many choices of things to do, that must be done, that she could choose none of them. She not only couldn't shift gears, her gears were locked. She was paralyzed into inaction and came to rely on other people to marshal her or just to do the task entirely instead of her. Her inability to initiate a simple motion read as extreme laziness. Inertia is my middle name, she was fond of saying to her worker.

This paralysis was stubborn and lingered for years, not months, after a hospital stay. She needed to be babied, but there was no one around to do it now, and her things just didn't get done. Slips of paper mounted, but filing terrified her and she didn't have a filing cabinet anyhow. She was as though blind, feeling under different clumps of stuff for half-remembered items. This mounding applied to clothing as well. Besides, she had lost her feel for the weather, and always wore the wrong thing.

She could not read. She could not write. She had been reading Dante's *Inferno* when first she went into the hospital, she remembered, and at quite a good clip too, but when she came out she couldn't even get down a fashion rag; the words bounced off her forehead like it was steel; she simply couldn't care about the contents of any written material, be it heavy or lightweight. Why? Why read it? Why absorb? This inability applied also to movies and video cassettes and computers and telephones; the latest amazing jumps in technology left her cold, and she could hardly turn on a radio, let alone program a VCR.

This left a huge gap in her time once filled by reading, writing, cinema. Nor could she hang out, she was getting too old, and she didn't have the money anyway. Her old habits of seclusion and screening out distraction remained, but there was nothing to be secluded for. Once in a while she prodded herself to write, but the old excitement of creation did not return, or if it did, it fizzled by morning after her nightly medication. It was a dry fuck, every word painful and laborious. But like sex itself, even masturbation, it was the initiative that was most lacking.

Her general state of indecision was matched only by her impatience. For example, waiting for doctors or nurses or clerks in the outpatient wing of the hospital was agony. She shifted from one leg to another like someone who was holding it in, and kept jabbing her face and her forms at personnel until they began to dismiss her as daffy. She could hardly sit still in a doctor's waiting room, a beauty parlor, or a church service, or stand in a postal queue, and travel was, forget it. She couldn't read, she was too nervous, she couldn't even watch TV. Instead she reverted to hospital behavior: long hours of blanking out, just watching the hands of the clock go round until the next mealtime or bedtime or wake-up time. Sometimes she panicked at the thought that she had thirty more years to kill this way, with only more and more institutionalization ahead of her and suicide no longer an option.

Perhaps due to the medication, her biggest trouble was she couldn't care about anything, and love was forgotten. That left getting through the blank days as comfortably as possible, trying not to sink under the boredom and total loss of hope. She was lucid, yes, at what price. She sometimes recognized on the faces of others joy and ambition and other emotions she could recall having had once, long ago. But her life was ruined, and she had no salvage plan. The decades were passing quickly and she was going gray; she was no longer attractive to anyone, male or female. Indeed, she felt herself repulsive, in the most literal sense. Hearing of a death, she often wished she could trade places with that person—let someone who knew how to organize and enjoy life benefit from her bodily health better than she could!

WELL-NOURISHED WHITE FEMALE

Could things ever be the same again between them, wondered Margaret. She had finished her sneak peek at the "Current Mental Status" form that her shrink had just filled out for her vocational testing under VESID. Axis schizophrenia, suicidal ideation, areas of weak impulse control: violence toward self. She guessed she had that coming. Judgment and Insight rated only fair to poor. Selective memory. But it was the Appearance that really made her wince: well-nourished white female with apparent tardive dyskinesia of the right arm and tongue. Couldn't she just call her fat or jowly and be done with it? God knows it was not nourishment, but empty bread. As for the tardive dyskinesia, it was a palsy she no longer even tried to control: her tongue felt feathery and her speech was often slurred. At times she spilled her orange juice in the mornings trying to pour it into a glass, and she had to stop smoking because her lack of control of her hand movements made it dangerous. She had practically forgotten how to type, even if she did not have tardive dyskinesia. She was a poor candidate for vocational training.

But worse than this realization was her sense of love-lessness. She let the form drop into her lap. She had thought, somehow, that her shrink loved her. When no one else could. Now where did she get that idea? A paid professional. And the form was so cold.

STABILIZED, YES

Dorrie had dressed up for the Concerned Care, Inc., Christmas party, because she knew it was the only Christmas party she would be invited to this year—but she was immediately disappointed at its soup kitchen flavor, the volunteers standing in lines behind the turkey and meat loaf, the gaudy decorations and Woolworth's sox under the tree, the down-and-out welfare look of the party crowd.

Well, at least they had a band for two hours. She was trying to learn the Macarena from her visiting nurse when she bumped into a face that was vaguely sinister and disturbing. "Don't I know you from somewhere?" He didn't look too sure of where he had met her either, but he introduced himself as Dr. Howie Bemis. Then suddenly she remembered: he was the doctor they had sent to put her in the hospital when she wasn't answering her phone or door last year. The scene came back to her: she pulling together all the command she possessed, refusing to answer his nosy questions, ordering him out of her apartment from the bed with her two fingers, "I cancelled Concerned Care, Inc., in writing months ago, now LEAVE my apartment, I order you to leave," and no sooner had she breathed a sigh of relief to get rid of him than the cops came, handcuffs, interrogations, injection, and the works, and as always she went into the hospital as "involuntary." That time it was only two months (and $300 missing from her purse).

By now it had dawned on him too. "So how are you doing?" He glanced approvingly at her outfit. "You look happy." She made a wry face: "Not quite." He tried again: "Content, at least?" She shook her head no. He finally settled on "Stabilized?"

"Stabilized, yes," she granted, glad to be rid of him.

I woke up one spring morning filled with light and peace and memories of Mark, a Russian fisherman's son from rural Maine whom I had not seen in over ten years. It was such a beautiful day, I thought, wouldn't it be great to plan a trip to see Mark again? I remembered that I had written to his old address in the city asking how he was and whether I could visit him. I was telephoned by a pleasant young fellow with a British accent who told me that Mark had long gone back to the country; and he gave me a rural route address. Since my letter had been intercepted and not forwarded, I was lazy about writing another one so quickly, just happy in knowing I could reach him when the time came.

Now the time was here. I fished for my white letter-writing pad and then I remembered I had used it up writing a will shortly before entering the hospital. I walked all the way to the stationery store and bought an identical pad after some searching. But when I got home and prepared to duplicate my heartfelt letter, I found that the precious address was not on my Rolodex. Nor was the city address I had used to obtain the other one. I searched my memory carefully until I recalled that fit of madness in which I had thrown out not just my pills but my papers and even my Rolodex files and address books in an effort to make a clean start.

I realized now that I might never see my friend Mark Petroff again, and whether he fared well or ill, was married or not, was still painting out there in Maine I would never know.

ORGONOMY

I read of a Reichian treatment once which was deemed successful: a seventy-nine-year-old widow began to recover "streaming" sensations in her body and limbs. Her cancer went into recession. But what should she do then? There was no one, nothing in her life for her to reach out toward. (Maybe this is why she had gotten sick in the first place— a cry for attention.)

THE MACROBIOTIC COOKING CLASS

Jos and her older sister, Meinke, were two beautiful married Dutch women who lived in the US who had signed up for Miriam Sepulveda's Macrobiotic Cooking class, held in her fifteenth-floor apartment overlooking Washington Square, where she and her husband Juan could watch the sun set behind the skyscrapers as they ate Miriam's carefully prepared macrobiotic meals. Meinke, Jos's older sister by ten years, looked equally handsome, made up, and well dressed except that she had a sagging jowl from a "yin condition" (too much sugar). (Every morning at 5:00 a.m. she arose to bake commercially profitable no-cholesterol muffins good for diabetics, her feet were killing her, and she looked forward to bedtime, "the best part of the day.") She had backpacked here from Europe for three months and had stayed for twenty-one years, marrying an Asian American; and she was followed by three out of four of her siblings. She had two daughters out in the suburbs, and was getting ready to put them through college.

Ruthie also was signed up to watch Miriam put together a full-course macrobiotic meal, observing the rather elaborate organic-cooking procedures adapted from Japanese tradition. Ruthie had been worried about a uterine growth which might be malignant. As Jos and Ruthie compared notes on what they knew of the health-giving qualities of macrobiotics, Jos told the story of Dirk, who had been dying of prostate cancer until he took up macrobiotic cooking, carrying his own utensils with him wherever he went. He not only got his cancer to go into remission, he sired two healthy children for whom he now cooked macrobiotically. He was forty-nine and he looked twenty-nine. Ruthie agreed that, from her own experience, macrobiotics seemed to halt the aging process. They checked out a picture on the back of his book showing Michio Kushi who (along with George Ohsawa) had originated macrobiotic cooking and founded healing centers around the world, and marveled at how trim, youthful, and energetic he appeared, though he must certainly be getting on in years. It works, they agreed. Then their conversation was cut short by the demands of the miso soup and the apple kanten.

The following week Ruthie enthusiastically took up where she and Jos had left off: "If only I could afford a cook, or to eat out at the macrobiotic restaurants every day (they have gotten expensive)," she said, "I would find it much easier to be fully macrobiotic—and after all, what good does partial do, on such a diet? But the elaborate organic shopping and cooking, especially to find all the cast iron ware and non-Teflon hand utensils required, is too much for me, and too expensive."

Jos then told of Dirk's friend, also with cancer, who had been wealthy enough to afford a private cook until the day he went back to "normal" eating.

"What happened?" Ruthie asked.

"He died of cancer," she said, with a peculiar half smile.

THE SLEEP ROOM

Lorraine, as a condition for getting into cooperative housing (there was a long wait in the hospital because there was a long waiting list), had to agree to go to a hospital day program so as to be out of the house all day. (The day program was supposed to prepare you for getting a proper job, but it didn't do it.)

All she knew for sure was that she missed her hospital bed, and further back, a room of her own where she could just crash and be beholden to nobody. All these pointless "activities" they made you do in the hospital in order to improve your status and get discharged were all repeated right here again in the day program—embarrassing juvenile quasi-activity which would have put a third grader to shame. Roll your head from side to side nine times, coloring to stay within the lines, making lists of what you were going to do with your free time and your nonexistent friends. Then there were great gaps of hours in your program with nothing structured in them, and you had to fill them as best you could, in the noisy plastic cafeteria where everyone ignored you and you didn't like them anyway.

Then she noticed on the directory a "lounge" and she checked it out: it was a tiny room with one dark-blue uncomfortable sofa on which there were usually three people sleeping upright in a sitting position like birds in a tree and one or two more on hard chairs. She began to go up to the lounge at every opportunity hoping to get a seat. At lunch hours it was usually filled with noisy white boys, who weren't trying to sleep at all, but just to eat and talk, but at other odd hours she sometimes lucked out and got a seat on the sofa, or, if she was, as often happened, crushingly disappointed, she just curled up in a ball on the floor next to the couch and slept on her jacket, so crunched she could barely be seen. She was comforted by the smell and presence of Blacks in the close quarters, those who were mostly there to sleep soundly for as long as they could.

She joined them wordlessly and became a fixture in the room. When activities were in session, she longed for the sleeping room where she could sleep off some of her medication (she was always tired, or else worn out from insomnia). Maybe they were all there for that reason.

But one day a sign was posted that due to the deplorable conditions in the "lounge" it was going to be converted into an office. Wouldn't you know. The one thing Lorraine had going for her to get through the day. She was so attached to her sleep regimen that she actually found herself haunting the room even after an Asian doctor or social worker put up his shingle, leaving the room only a crack open. She just couldn't believe her sleep room had been taken away from her just like that, with no possible substitute. And she was so tired.

TWO NECKLACES

Donna didn't care for crafts at all, but the quality of the beads attracted her. White porcelain with splashes of gay color—oranges, pinks, purples—they reminded her of those Dutch flower candies of her youth, so she attempted a necklace, and then added another strand and closed them with an X clasp. She made them long enough for a teacher to wear to work over a nice dress, with the hopes that one day she would work again.

This happened. So that when Donna wore them she got a good idea for crafts: she encased all the pills she had ever been on in the little bubble plastic shells children's bubblegum charms came in, and strung them together in varying sizes and colors and shapes, and that was a lot of pills and a lot of variety. Her weirdo necklace. Then she went off medication entirely.

That's how Donna ended up wearing her weirdo necklace in the hospital, on relapse, to impress her OT instructor. Donna didn't know if she would ever again have the chance to add her new medications to the necklace, because it was too difficult to get the charm casings—and the liquid plastic to frame the pills in the casings with Latin names stenciled in tiny colored computer lettering—from inside the hospital.

Rachel had been hospitalized six times in ten years, staying an average of four months per stay, sometimes longer, sometimes shorter, but all of them involuntary. (She never stayed longer than six months, because this was roughly coincident with the lapse of Medicaid for short-term hospital care, and efforts by the hospital to put her care on a sounder financial footing; and it was usually in this interim that she took advantage of the lull to escape.) Every time she went in, especially after the first, she felt submerged, as if someone were holding her under water for months. When she came out she was fat, help-less, unable to make the smallest decision, speechless, and thoroughly programmed by the rigid hospital routine, so that even her stomach grumbled on time, at precisely 5:00 p.m. And she fell asleep wherever she was at 11:00 p.m., like clockwork. She felt so imprisoned that had she had a calendar she would have scratched off the days (except that her date of discharge was always unresolved until its sudden announcement toward the end, when everything speeded up).

She always made a point of going in as involuntary—wheelchairs, police breaking in the door (sometimes up to ten men at once), EMS ambulances and police cars, handcuffs and injections, the whole bit—not because she liked it, nor because (after her first time) she thought it would do any good legally to get her out (and it was a sure ticket to second-class status inside the hospital itself), but just for honor's sake. She was involved in major resistance, refusal of medication, paperwork, hearings, from the start, and it usually took two months to break her, that is, to convince her that denying the grounds for arrest wasn't going to work again, and she'd have to start to work her way out, in other words, kiss ass.

LOVING THE HOSPITAL

Mrs. Brophy's only vacations were her prolonged hospital stays and she didn't know how she could ever have gone without them. She felt that only then could she hit bottom and stay there (until they started pestering her for release). Though in reality it was never as good as she fantasized when she was out and juggling the cares and worries of a large family, she imagined it as a twenty-four-hour cocoon where one didn't even have to bother giving orders or managing a staff, because personnel just did everything by themselves like some wound-up robots. Unlike certain bored patients who envied the ever-busy hospital staff their work, and volunteered to make their own beds, she luxuriated in having her bed made by a hospital team (even if they had to wake her at seven to throw her out of bed to do it), in having a lunch tray with her name on it on the cart always rolling in at the same time every day (even if it was always the same thing, cheese/bread in a variety of rehashings, and not exactly waiter service:

standing in line in one's robe), and in having roommates to chat with and a community room to play in (though she could never master Ping-Pong, and the TV, when you could hear it at all over the piano and the talking, was usually on a Spanish channel or about something violent). The one thing that really got to her, though, was the pay telephones in the hall that were always tied up and usually without even a chair to sit on. If only she could have a private TV and a private telephone line, surely she would never think of leaving. And even so, promptings for her to leave the hospital were always met with her subtle resistance.

And once the initial Welcome Home had been exhausted of any love or care therein (and that tended to diminish every time she was put away afresh, and the phrase "in and out of hospitals" began to stick to her) and it all became too much for her again, then she began to long for the hospital to bottom out in.

So much so that she began to find excuses to hang around in the general vicinity of Beth Abraham. For instance, she was much attracted to the Greek diner across the street from her old Ward 17—the Ambrosia. There you could get the best homemade vanilla ice cream in nice ice cream glasses, something they never had in the hospital, which is why they sometimes took you there for a twenty-minute "treat." She always knew she was nearing another hospital stay by the frequency with which she went to the Ambrosia for a "treat"—and hang the kids.

On this particular day, she limited herself to one scoop (only $1.20 plus tip, but it came in a saucer, not even a metal ice cream dish) and she couldn't even prolong her sitting time because there was a terrible drilling noise coming from the front of the restaurant where they were redesigning the entrance under a cloak of black tarpaulins.

The Y at Sixty-Third Street

Why is everything around here so damned expensive?, Cyndi wondered, I can't even afford a banana at Melissa's Gourmet Deli. Must be Lincoln Center nearby, a tourist trap. For dinner she spent three dollars in a Pizza Hut in a nearby basement soon to be closed, and hoped her ICM (Intensive Case Management) worker, that is Tommasina (Tommy for short) would reimburse her when she saw her. When. She waited all week and a half for her one hour social work visit, her only contact with humanity, while she waited for her apartment to be made livable, something Tommy had promised had already happened before her hospital discharge date which was weeks ago already. If only I had some spending money, it wouldn't be so bad up here, Cyndi thought. But I can't even go to the park, it's too cold. It was March of a cold and slushy winter, and the ground in the park was wet and even the benches were wet, as Cyndi found out when she dragged her one blanket out the Y door 6:00 a.m. one morning when she couldn't sleep. Trying at least to enjoy that she was assigned to an uptown neighborhood near Central Park. There was exactly one chair where you checked in your keys, an awful orange-fiberglass handmade chair that looked like a slanted box.

Other than that she sat in front of a missionary building, an imposing not a welcoming place, hoping for a handout.

In addition to trying for a good sandwich with a drink when her ICM worker came to visit, Cyndi had copped a massage for her nervous strain that she got waiting all this time for her own place to live. She knew Tommy was gay. The massage touched her. She was surprised at the feeling, now that hadn't happened in a long time. She became aware of her loneliness, how cut off she was. She needed the touch of another human being. She doubted even getting a permanent place of her own would help. Her social life had died while she was incarcerated. Just what was she supposed to do all day. I'll be damned if I'll go to a day program. That would be to become a permanent patient. And I'll never get a job now. Or if I got one, I couldn't hold it. Cyndi lay on her bed wishing for a visit from her social worker. She hoped she could maneuver another massage this time, which was really off the books.

The Y on Thirty-Fourth Street

The only good thing about the big old tall building near Ninth Avenue that the Y had taken over temporarily to increase its space for accommodations was the hot showers with big old-fashioned nozzles and the price for a room: thirty dollars per night. That was about as cheap as you could get in New York, especially near Penn Station, and that's why a lot of foreign students inhabited the building.

But the room. The room was as small and barren as Van Gogh's, though a good deal less tasteful. Everything was tacky and stuffy at the same time, and what were you supposed to do in there? masturbate? with the background music the constant sound of the slamming doors of the foreign students returning from their showers; but there was no socializing allowed in the bedrooms and no place else to socialize.

The most interesting thing in walking distance was the outdoor shopping district on Ninth Avenue where you could find a whole skinned pig hanging, if you wanted one, its terrified head still on. And all kinds of spices and stuff from the Mideast, all dirt cheap, the only trouble was there were no cooking facilities at the Y and no one to cook with or for. (He settled for a bar of Greek olive oil soap to use in his next hot shower—which were over-frequent, to take advantage of the one luxe aspect of the accommodations.) Gene would have liked to pretend he was Lawrence Durrell living in Africa but the truth was he was in New York City, in the belly of the beast, a user and substance abuser who was on a waiting list for Phoenix House: a detoxification center first and then a halfway house were being lined up, in the meantime what should he do with himself? There was exactly one rickety chair in his room, an uncomfortable small bed, and some blowy curtains with turquoise daisies on them. He was high up but there was no view from his small window, the walls were thick, closet space barely adequate for his few belongings which he determined to leave behind, a vest or two in a large swimming bag he used as a small suitcase. He still didn't know what he was going to do if that detox center didn't come through quick; he had been without a fix too long already and some borrowed methadone—well, you just couldn't kick that way.

But the long day, breaking in his new room, was nothing compared with the night. By ten o'clock Gene was frantic with the itch for a fix or at least some methadone, a cigarette maybe? something, anything. He went down the elevator out into the street, which had a wild crazy energy of its own this far west. Too bad he was a doper not a drinker and out of money anyway, or maybe he could sit in a bar if he could find one. Gene made a desperate phone call or two out there on the street corner, it was already eleven and pitch black and menacing around here, but it was one of those nights, he was too far away from his connections and his own haunts and street routines and he couldn't even score some methadone to keep the panic at bay.

LOSERS

ELLIS MARTIN SHEEN

Ellis Martin Sheen was a short paunchy Irishman with an angry bloom of red splotches all over his skin, even covering his head up through his bald pate like a pattern of primroses. He went to his "groups" at the CDTP (Continuing Day Treatment Program), contributing the minimum, as most do, revealing (in Diet and Nutrition) that he lived on food stamps, essentially eating out of cold cans, say a can of Veg-All over a can of Dinty Moore's beef stew.

Then one day he began to challenge everyone in every group he went to: "Have you ever seen me take a drink? Have you ever heard me even talk about it??" It appeared that his social worker, Greg Mueller, apparently needing a handy pigeonhole to account for Martin's emotional illness, had decided that Martin was an alcoholic.

Martin reiterated: "I don't go to parties where people bring six-packs every Saturday night, and I certainly don't drink alone, I haven't got the money even if I wanted to. What's he talking about? Has anyone here ever seen me drinking? Has anyone heard me even talking about it??"

LEON FELDSHER

Leon Feldsher was fifty-nine years old and lived in Herbert Danziger Houses, a low-income city housing project for the elderly and the disabled. Not quite old enough for social security, and unable to get early retirement, he qualified for disability by virtue of mental distress, and though no one was quite sure just which psychiatric ailment he had (bipolar stress disorder or paranoid schizophrenia didn't seem correct), that he was clinically depressed no one could possibly deny.

Once a week he also qualified for a homemaker home health aide (HHHA) to do the heavy chores like laundry and mopping. In this case, it was Carmela Santos, and she had just brought up the laundry from the in-house laundromat, which was cheaper than one on the street, but still too expensive. (Since she did all his bedding and towels every time, and used bleach yet, it was always over five dollars, sometimes way over.) "How you feel?" she had asked, her bottom jaw way out with her dentures (she was about his age, give or take a few years). She fixed herself some Maxim's freeze-dried coffee with the dried milk substitute she had to bring in herself since he hadn't got milk.

She had remade his bed, and he switched back from the armchair to the bed gratefully. She was in the kitchen preparing to mop the floor. It was harder now that they had taken Mex, an industrial mopping agent, off the market. Now she had to use a mix of Soilax and ammonia (in itself hard to find at reasonable prices).

Leon was still mulling the question "How you feel?" (it was rare anyone ever asked him a direct question anymore) and his own answer, "Not so good today." Why not, she had wanted to know, and he could only gesture in the direction of his small army of pills. Why then, should I feel guilty, he thought, like I didn't when I had my leg in a cast. Guilty of not being really sick, only unhappy. For which you don't get paid. Unhappy and unloved.

He burrowed deeper under the covers till he was under the bottom quilt. I feel sick, why shouldn't I lay in bed all day.

He called Carmela. "Can I ask you something?"

"What is it," she wanted to know.

"Will you give me a hug?"

Muttering something about her husband, still she engulfed him in her aproned bosom, her face even made up could not lose its wrinkles, and she smelled like the cleaning lady.

ALBA AND EVA

"My heart was really with Eva, you know," said Alba, my ICM worker. "It really was. But what could I say? Just get dressed, I said, and here she's telling me she's afraid to die. She's all alone, you know. I'm afraid to die, she says, and I say, Get dressed, we're going to the Water Street Settlement to enroll you in a program.

"But once we got there, Ms. Calderon, who's in charge of the program, didn't stay fifteen minutes into the interview, which was pretty exhaustive, they had Eva there all day just asking every kind of question, they wore us out, and at the end of that time Ms. Calderon, who had hardly even been present, returned to say Eva wasn't qualified, you know, dismissed on a technicality they probably caught the first fifteen minutes, but went on with the interview anyway.

"I don't know," sighed Alba, "I do my best for them, but what do I tell her now when she says she's all alone and afraid to die?"

"PREVOC"

Brian McNair needed a little job off the books. To cover the rise in his rent. He lived on base minimum SSI for mental disability, and he heard you could work up to $80/mo. (and thereafter they could take half out of your wages) but he was loathe to get involved with government red tape for an itsy-bitsy job, and he was afraid it would endanger his benefits by showing he could work after all.

He maybe wished for a job, but he knew he couldn't handle one. But the other alternative was to lose his cheap apartment and have to go into "supportive" housing, with assigned roommates, and state control of him and his finances, right down to a weekly "allowance."

So he signed up at St. George's Hospital Day Program, hoping to get some vocational training. But the very beautiful social worker in charge of vocational—Julie Sachs, who reminded him of his sister's camp counselor that he once had a crush on, with her hard lean body in well-fitting pants and perfectly applied makeup and dark wavy hair with bangs—told him he would have to be in the hospital program first. She embarrassed him by asking if he bathed with soap, and explained that many mental patients couldn't be bothered to bathe regularly with soap or to use deodorant, and these were the sort of things you had to have down before they could track you into "prevoc."

Brian figured he had almost nine months left on his lease before the rent heat came down for real, so he signed on at St. George's Hospital. Which was a complete and total waste, except that it got him out of the house every day, where he had been prone to blank out or sleep as much as possible. Instead he hassled with red tape worse than college registration to get into "groups" where nothing much was discussed, and in the long stretches between groups he laid out on the benches and tried to sleep, until a guard caught him. Then he sat in the hospital lobby counting his change to see if he could afford a candy bar or he listened in on hospital conversations about goiter or hernia operations and the like.

Eventually he proved himself to Julie Sachs, by writing a piece for her gazette group about the loss of his dog during his hospitalization. Then he had to be interviewed for "prevoc" and come up with a résumé, though he had scarcely worked in the past ten years. He wore a sweater that his cousin gave him that looked new and he dug up an old résumé that he had once made up as an exercise in the hospital. He didn't know what he was going to do if he failed to get into "prevoc." He couldn't stand much more of the hospital day program. The people in "prevoc" had a certain determination about them. They all looked normal. He really wanted, needed to get in. And he made it.

Once in, he had to take a lot of tests. His math proved to be at a fifth-grade level. There went VESID, the government job-training program for office work! But no, Sara Saffir, the sweet, bright "prevoc" instructor, assured him, he could study remedial math and take the test at VESID later on. The end of his lease loomed. He didn't think it would be so easy to make up years of math that way, but she gave him a workbook and he dutifully went to work on his fractions and decimals. He answered the questions for a while, by checking against the answer key—there was no tutor, and Sara was usually in private conference with one or another in the group; only rarely did she come around to bail him out. But when he arrived at decimals he came up against a stone wall. From then on he only pretended to be at work on his math. Once or twice she caught him dozing over his book.

He decided to change books: *What Color Is Your Parachute?* looked good, a bestseller on job hunting. But all he could determine from it was that résumés didn't do it, that you needed to start your own business, and it helped if you had a home computer.

He began to look forward to his turn on the computer, when he could practice his typing on a program called Mavis Beacon: there was actually a human voice that reproved or congratulated you on your score. When he got up to thirty WPM, he implored Sara to put him on Windows 95, Microsoft Word 6.1 (because he knew with his poor math he would never make the VESID computer-training program, even if there had been time for it before his lease ran out). On that program he stumbled about, clicking his mouse negligently, until he was more or less able to copy a page out of a book, say of résumés.

Meanwhile the pressure was on to do volunteer work; a month of this was a necessary requirement to prove to VESID that you could last on a job before they bothered to train you. Brian had already given up inwardly on VESID because of the math, and because he knew they had a dated WordPerfect 5.1 program that conflicted with what he had just taught himself on the computer. But he called the pound and volunteered to walk the dogs; he felt sorry for them all cooped up as he himself had been in the hospital. He felt even more compassionate toward them when he realized from the time they were brought in most of them had only three weeks to live.

He realized from comparing notes with his classmates that he was lucky to get even a callback. Even volunteer work was hard to come by. They tried him out for a day, but he wasn't fast enough in decaging and leashing the dogs for a walk of only half a block (not even long enough for the dog to shit on the street instead of in his small cage). Only the larger dogs got walked at all, and only if the attendant felt like it, not on a regular basis. Brian's heart bled over one poor black hound who was sick and afraid, too morose to even enjoy a walk out of his cage. Brian wanted to adopt him, but his apartment was too small for such a big dog, and he couldn't afford to feed him.

By the time his lease ran out—freeze!—Brian was waiting for the Asia Society to call him back on a volunteer afternoon a week filing for the fundraising office. His rent was going up fifty dollars per month and he was no closer to getting a paying job of any kind. He was barely able to understand the high-tech want ads, let alone qualify for them. And then there was his pretend résumé, and his lack of a wardrobe. And on his medication he didn't feel strong enough for manual labor and he was too out of touch to find it.

He figured he would just keep paying what he could on his rent until he got the eviction notice and then he would stop paying altogether, and save his money for the streets. He guessed he had better inform his caseworker that he needed a supportive housing arrangement, because he knew there was a waiting list.

The question was whether or not he could or should stay in "prevoc." It gave him somewhere to go and something to do that was a bit better than the hospital day treatment program. He felt that the people around him had "goals," and he admired them, though he hadn't made a friend in either program. But he was running out of things to do in the class, and volunteer work was not what he had had in mind. How long did they let you stay in "prevoc" before they started asking questions about "voc"?

INCONTINENCE

Mrs. Rafferty's worst fear was that she would end up having to wear diapers (the kind she had seen in a TV commercial, with broad sides in plastic for the rivulets to flow into, like some kind of oversize menstrual pad, except that she was postmenopausal) and be unable to go out into the street because she couldn't control it. As it was, it seemed she had to urinate all the damned time, not much of a trickle, maybe, but enough pressure was there that she was afraid she'd wet herself or worse, embarrass herself by a gush to the ground. She took to wearing slacks just in case, better to change your pants than to leave a puddle. Yet it never actually happened, though she felt her once-excellent control loosening and she worried awfully about long subway rides and had to take taxis she couldn't afford for fear of public shame.

What did happen, though, cruel joke on her, was that she found herself shitting in her pants while walking on the street. Though she applied maximum pressure to ringtight her anus, nothing could prevent the initial poop, and her slacks were soon covered with a large stain in the rear. She hurried home, unable to believe what was happening, and just made it home in time to shit out the rest (a lot), wash herself and her legs repeatedly, and change clothes, rinsing the soiled pants again and again.

THE MARCH FRACTURE

Marlene had kneecap trouble, shriveling cartilage in the joints, which ruined her whole life. She couldn't go out anymore, except to function in her immediate housing (Rosner Co-ops). She leaned too heavily on her husband and lost him. She lost all kinds of friends. Because she couldn't go out anymore. Subways with their strange passageways and often formidable stairways were out of the question, and buses didn't run regularly enough. She smoked heavily, ate a no-salt diet, and drowned herself in medications. Her finances on disability and what she could squeeze from a divorce were precarious.

And then one day things got worse. She broke into an uncontrollable scream in Sloan's Supermarket, aisle 5. She had fractured the interset of bones above the arch in her right foot, something soldiers did on long marches. (It also happened to be the month of March, quite coincidentally.) According to her foot doctor (a twenty-dollar taxi ride uptown) it was unrelated to her crippled condition in general.

Now she was really grounded. Neighbors offered to go to the store for her and they did so once or twice and not again. (Nina, her next-door neighbor, had a foot condition of her own.) She took to paying a little neighbor girl to go down to the store and order things to go back up with a delivery boy; but she couldn't afford to continue it. Attempts to collar stray visitors into doing her shopping, even with delivery boy, did not work: she lassoed a quart or two of milk and a *TV Guide* at best. She could no longer show off her cooking, and her food stock had run out anyhow. Finally she was forced to fall back on her home attendant, who could barely speak English, and she was urged to stock up really, not just to get milk and a couple of pears. Because she often went hungry when the food ran out. She tried to get more hours from a home attendant but this request got swallowed in red tape because a march fracture was deemed a temporary condition. As for keeping up with newspapers and *TV Guide*, forget it. She had six to eight weeks to go and any improvement had been minuscule. What if it didn't heal at all? She took comfort from a saying of the doctor's that no matter what you did, right or wrong, cast or no cast, crutches or cane, it would heal anyway and be even stronger than before. But she was well over fifty and menopausal. Even though she drank a lot of milk, osteoporosis might be setting in. The thought recurred, What if it doesn't heal?

THE VISIT

Martha Ritter was on time for her visit to her old friend Elizabeth Haas. It had been a long time. Martha had been in another city; Elizabeth, who was seventy-seven, had lost her husband; and there was much water under the bridge since their last meeting.

Martha rang again. She was there on the dot, at exactly the agreed-upon time, what could be the matter? Could Elizabeth have gone out to the store?

She decided to wait, even though there was no seat anywhere in the long hallway, just a large potted plant next to an open window in front of Elizabeth's next-door neighbor. She tried leaning on the sill, which was shallow, but she didn't want to try the potted plant for fear of getting her skirt dirty.

Fifteen minutes ticked away. Maybe she wasn't at the store at all, but just didn't hear the ring. Martha banged on the door as loud as she could. Still nothing.

In the end she just camped out on the floor in front of the apartment, banging and ringing periodically. It was better than leaning against the potted plant.

Forty-five minutes passed. At last Martha had had it. She decided to arouse the next-door neighbor and perhaps put in a phone call.

Luckily for her the next-door neighbor was in, and receptive. "Perhaps she just didn't hear you," she volunteered. "Come in and have a seat. I saw someone sitting out there all the time and didn't know what to make of it. Here's the telephone, I'll call her."

When she finally opened the door, Elizabeth did not seem too contrite at what she had put her friend through. She explained offhandedly that her hearing was going. The television had been on. Evidently she didn't receive many visitors anymore.

Martha panicked *for* her, especially when she found more evidence of hearing loss: she had to enunciate every word clearly or Elizabeth didn't get it. Would anybody bother with the long wait Martha had just been through? Would they think of calling her from next door (because it was a big housing complex and to find the nearest street phone would be a journey)? Would she herself be up for trying this all over again?

Perhaps a phone call would do. But unfortunately it was hard to reach Elizabeth by phone as well; she had an answering machine and seldom returned calls. (She had only picked up this time because they had a prearranged date and Elizabeth had been wondering what was taking Martha so long.)

Martha was worried for her friend Elizabeth. She was seventy-seven and she shrugged off seeing a doctor about a hearing aid. Who would try to get through to see her now?

STANLEY MOSS

I had known Stanley so long I couldn't remember where or when I had met him, but certainly it was after I came to New York in 1967. He had been on Elavil, an antidepressant, since 1963—who knows what he would have been like without it?

As it was, he was a great bullfrog of a man—dressed in stained suits, with beret and scarf and glasses—who liked to eat meat chops out every night at Greek diners on his philosophy professor's pay from a small suburban college; and I joined him maybe once a week or every ten days when he came downtown from his overstuffed apartment near Columbia University, his alma mater. Once in a while we went to a movie of his esoteric choice, but not often. Mostly he was interested in used books, used books and records, and sometimes objets d'art from, say, Thailand, and he could go on for hours about them to his few friends, like a little boy with trading cards. His apartment looked like a used bookshop and there was literally barely enough room to sit down, but he kept on buying more, causing him to be short of cash at the end of every month. (He would spend seventy dollars a shot for a bag of books, or an objet d'art, which were not, in my opinion, of the highest quality.) He also liked to gossip about old friends, many of whom had passed out of his life and few of whom I had ever met, and to this end he had honed his conversation.

What we did *not* discuss was his magnum opus on which he had spent eight years and every free hour, and which ran into almost a thousand pages. Once I asked to see it, and he showed me a chapter. It was a philosopher's look at love, but (I have often regretted) I was put off by page 2, a long argument asserting that Marx was madly in love with his wife Jenny. I did not read any further, not understanding what difference this made in any serious philosophical argument.

One day he called me to meet him at the Tenth Street Deli in my neighborhood for matzoh ball soup. He had kept me informed of his attempts to get the book published through Howard Zukofsky, a rather prominent former radical who was now well established and well connected. Now he took a letter from his jacket pocket and showed it to me. It was from NYU Press, and rather self-consciously well written. "Thank you for sharing your MS with us through Howard Zukofsky," it began, but noting its "awesome" labors and a formal training in philosophy "I could not follow," it ended by advising him to trim and edit and focus more, and suggested he try another press, "as we do not do philosophy titles here."

"I'm sorry," I said, handing the letter back to Stanley, and taking a gulp of water. He was on his meat sandwich, and he muttered, almost under his breath, "What do I do now?" Zukofsky had been his ace in the hole, and we both knew that Duke University and the other presses mentioned would not even bother to read the book, let alone publish it.

Charlene had had two marriages and four children, now grown, and all she had to show for it was a serious bladder infection. She rented a small house in Bath, Maine, that she shared with her mother Berenice. Berenice was seventy-eight and apt to refer to herself as the "bionic woman" she had so many false parts (just as blowzy blond Charlene referred to herself ironically as "white bread"). But Berenice kept herself up well, she had a charming short blond wig and her bulging stomach (presumably from a McDonald's habit) was well disguised in her neat clothes. She drove a little yellow sports car with which she visited her other daughter Brenda (who was just splitting with her husband and having child-custody problems with her daughter Jennifer). Berenice got alimony from Al, her former husband, but it wasn't enough to pay for her shopping sprees, evidence of which decorated the bathroom and her own room with a thousand little touches of her "taste"—the pigeon blood roses trim on her towels, for example, or her Japanese cat pictures in the living room.

So to make ends meet, she did what her daughter did, became a "care provider" and companion. And wasn't she lucky that Cleo Sonnenberg, a former fourth-grade teacher, came wandering right onto her lawn, complaining that she was afraid to sleep alone since her husband died and would pay a small fortune for Berenice to sleep over on weekday nights, and attend to her modest needs. And so began an increasingly encroaching relationship which some months later Berenice wanted to end.

Yet she still had to comb her mailbox every day anxiously looking for Al's check which was always "in the mail." (She didn't like to call him up about it all the time, and sweated it out instead. Sometimes she was driven to such despair that she called the post office as soon as it opened, demanding to go through the mail herself.)

But still she began talking about ending her companion status, as if to build up her courage. Every evening as she left for work she told Charlene that today would be the day she would bring it up to Cleo, and every morning upon her return she had to confess that she hadn't had the heart to end it. One time it was the anniversary of Cleo's husband's death and Cleo was terribly down. And another time Cleo had made a beautiful spread with ham and everything, so Berenice just felt it would be ungrateful—in fact, she invited Cleo to Charlene's dinner party that same week.

Meanwhile Charlene was putting in more and more time with her own clients, Jojo and Clara. Her path seldom collided with her mother's since she had a day shift and her mother a sleepover. She was apt to say that, wheelchair disabilities and all, her clients still had what it took to be happy: friends and money. Whereas Berenice expressed pity whenever she talked about Cleo: "that poor thing." (She never let you guess that she was even older and lonelier than her client.)

And I guess Berenice is there still, sleeping over at Cleo Sonnenberg's, afraid to break the news that this paid-for companionship is over. (For whom is she most afraid, for Cleo or for herself?)

Pauline was eighty-two and suffering from something worse than infirmity. She was a paranoid who barely avoided permanent institutionalization because she was from a wealthy well-educated background and had once been a noted pianist. She saw a therapist two or sometimes three times a week. Her doctor was Jewish, with a large drawing of Freud hanging on his wall, and he told her something interesting from the Old Testament (where did he get *that*, from *Moses and Monotheism*?): that old King Saul, the first king of the Jews, had been a paranoid who had first employed the shepherd David as a harpist to relieve his symptoms of exaggerated fear and suspiciousness. (That his fear was self-fulfilling and David went on to become Saul's replacement as king is another subject.) The point was that music is good for the ailing soul, especially for paranoia, which maybe the Jews were prone to, considering their historical persecutions, especially under Hitler.

While not encouraged to play piano anymore—she had sold her piano—Pauline did not need to be told to listen to good music. She had listened to WNCN until that station went out of business, the last good classical music station in the New York area. But then her doctor suggested radio station WISS (99.9 on her dial) as a substitute.

Now Pauline had an old heavy stereo set with a built-in FM radio and a huge collection of LPs. But she seldom could get up to change the records since she was as if glued to her lounge chair; so she got out of the habit of using the stereo. And the FM radio was no prize. Someone had stepped on the cord to the speaker and the sound was frazzled; it waxed and it waned.

Nonetheless Pauline began to leave the radio on from 11:00 a.m. till 10:00 p.m. when she retired for the night. It made her feel less lonely; and the walls of sound washing over her were soothing as the sound of ocean breakers. She reported to her doctor that radio station WISS really did help her, and he was pleased.

But no sooner had she somewhat recovered from her recent hospitalization, in which she had almost been left in the old folks' wing for good (a major scare), than she began to find fault with the station. There was too much advertising, aimed at the middle class, consumers of Lincoln Center extravaganzas and Broadway musicals and fancy French midday restaurants and air travel and most of all medical and financial advice. She would be listening along only to be torn out of her reverie by a barker announcing a countdown on a Persian-carpet sale, only two days left.

And listening to what? It was some minor master she would need a historical chart to find as often as it was Bach or Beethoven. And the announcers seemed to take a perverse delight in inflicting on their listeners the truly bad music of some forgotten maestro while shortchanging them on Mozart or Haydn by playing only a short piece, or a single movement of a long one; somehow, the announcers managed to put only a dollop of truly good sound in the mix to keep her listening—and when she slugged through all those advertisements and preliminary pieces for the promised Mozart, it was over before she turned around. Pauline felt cheated.

She couldn't beat it. If she tried to plug in only once in a while to catch the good stuff, she invariably got the tail end of some Mozart divertimento, followed by a whole rash of advertising or weak works. There was no way to turn it off and on, she just had to suffer through the bad part. (As far as she knew there was no program guide, and even if there was she was not up to the effort to track it down.)

Was it true what she read that the age group of classical music lovers began at fifty now, and that the audience was dying out? She didn't understand why they had to play the same old war horses over and over when there were literally hundreds of works to choose from, say, even in the oeuvre of the short-lived Schubert. Or why they preferred Tchaikovsky and Dvořák to Handel and Haydn.

Eventually her irritation became so frequent and the good pieces so rare that she turned it off for longer and longer periods. And finally she turned it off altogether.

Then she had just the drip-drip of the kitchen faucet to listen to, that couldn't be repaired.

THE LAST DATE

Lynn waited at an outdoor table at Sforza's coffeehouse in the Village for her date to show. He was supposed to be there at 6:00 p.m. He had insisted on the location, not she; she didn't much care for Sforza's of late, it was empty and dingy. She was sitting out on the corner of the block where Sullivan crosses Bleecker, and she had plenty of time to watch the local mafia action at the table directly in front of her: a couple of intense Russian turtleneck types who gave her the eye were followed by (after they had left) a cop car sitting on the corner next to the café for a full fifteen minutes as though apprised of an undercover rendezvous (but missed it all the same); and some half hour later a little Russian Jew, a straggler, looked for the two Russians in vain, missing both them and the cop car.

She was watching all this action in between glancing at her watch and the Russian waitress, who was peremptory. "I'm waiting for someone," muttered Lynn once again to the waitress (who was a small-faced, long-legged blond) without ordering.

She told herself she was about to leave—Neil never been so late—when she saw him across the street rushing down the wind toward her, papers under his arm, looking very professorial.

She straightened up as he slipped his skinny torso into the small ice-cream chair across from her. "So you were about to leave were you? How late am I?" he asked offhandedly, and didn't bother to wait for the answer. "I met a woman."

Lynn ordered a house coffee with whipped cream, her usual. Neil ordered a double espresso, iced. It seemed he had just had dinner and the woman, a Bulgarian music student, had given him her card. "It's a pity, I just ran out of my own cards," he added.

Lynn knew they were only friends, but she could not help feeling insulted. As if she were not a woman herself. He always did this, bored her with his tales of attempted pickups which never panned out. Sometimes he placed ads for secretarial help just to get a date.

What was his trouble? Was it that he was in therapy with two different therapists, a male and a female, and he went on and on with anyone else just as though he were in analysis? She listened to him dutifully, sometimes grateful that she didn't have to speak. He didn't seem to know the difference between a monologue and a conversation. He questioned her perfunctorily about her own life only after long soliloquies, and then launched into another one.

When at last it was time to go, he bared his wallet: empty. Then he asked if he could borrow a twenty or better yet fifty bucks to get through the month. Lynn said she didn't have it on her, taking out what she did have, a ten. He clipped the bill from her wrist and paid for both of them with it. With a certain smugness he said, "At last you're paying for my coffee for a change." She felt bruised, it wasn't fair. She never ordered more than one coffee to his three, and besides he usually ordered dinner only for himself. (She ordered only a side plate of coleslaw at most, or nibbled at his bread.) She wanted to remind him that his salary was at least six times her disability check, but she said nothing.

On the way back, he said he did not want to walk through the park again; last time it had depressed him. He was drawn to scout a bookshop nearby, and she said she would pass on that.

Somehow she knew he would never call again, and he did not. Neither did she want to call him.

Cherie's wedding was the occasion of the first gathering of the clan in thirty years. Because she was the first grand-child of Greta to get married. (And Greta was seventy-nine and wanted to be a great-grandmother before her days were done.) What a bride's bride Cherie made, with her soft pouty face and full lips and curly flaxen bob! And her expensive dress with its shapely tiny buttons and long train. She was old fashioned and fashionable too, European and American both.

Aunt Matilde (Mattie for short) was the eldest of Greta's three daughters and she had never married. She was rumored to be mentally incompetent and that was pretty much true. She had just arrived at the Marriott flustered and unkempt, an embarrassment to everyone, and here she was looking for her mother.

"She's in room 2018 having her wig done right," said Cherie's mother, Helene, who had to keep tab of things both large and small. Helene was organized, as one had to be running a large family. "Why don't you go up there too, you're scheduled for a makeup job. Ask for Joanne, she's very good, you'll see."

"But I don't wear makeup," protested Mattie weakly. (She had already been overruled on the jewelry question earlier, when her mother had come up with a set of pearls with matching clip-on earrings to relieve the starkness and bad taste of her all-black outfit—to a wedding!)

"You're wearing makeup tonight," said Helene determinedly. Then, wheedling, "Don't you want to come out good in the family portrait tonight? It'll be the first one in over twenty-five years of the Grubach family together—minus Papa of course, may he rest in peace. But we had to schedule it separately from the wedding photo session, because Ernst and Karen just got in to the airport from Tampa and it'll take them a while to check in and dress."

So that's how Matilde found herself in the makeup chair being makeup-based and powdered, and mascaraed for under her glasses—but it was the drawing of the Clara Bow lips that really made her uptight. (It's true that her lip line was not distinctly enough demarcated, but still.) When at last she put back on her glasses and saw herself in the mirror, she freaked. "Mutti, I look embalmed!" She could just feel all that cement eating into her wide-open pores. She looked ten years older.

But Greta had her own troubles: the photo man had called her "Grandma" when routinely asking her to shift her position. She felt this had been familiar and rude at the same time.

It was nearly time for the wedding when the Grubach family got together for their portrait: three boys and three girls who hadn't been together in one room for almost thirty years. In addition to the wide disparity in their ages and educations, each had gone his own way, and only Mattie was still dependent on their mother. They had barely two words to say to each other, but every one of them valued the portrait enough to get there on time.

It was a hastily put together, small and drafty room, and George, the youngest boy, who was about thirty-six now, with a growing family, paced the room nervously. "I just saw the photographer outside. He said he would be in here in a minute."

The photographer had been suitably rebuked by the bride's father for calling Greta "Grandma" and now he was in confusion about the ages and descent of the others, whom he had gone to some pains to get straight. If Greta was not Grandma, then maybe she was Great-Grandma and Mattie, who was already gray, was Grandma. Certainly they had begun to look alike in old age.

Finally, in the heat of the moment, he cast aside such reflections and lined up the women under the chin of Vicki (Victoria), the youngest and most vivacious, and Mattie ended up in the shadow of her mother Greta, and her sister Helene.

Sandra had the window seat on the cut-rate jet at Horizon Airlines. There had been a driving cold winter rain that morning when she set out, and she was glad she had made a prior appointment with car service to JFK, glad for the opportunity to board early and even some kind of promise that if everyone showed in time they might leave earlier than 10:00 a.m. (but as it was, they left a half an hour later).

A young Black cadet came on and sat in the aisle seat one seat away from her. She watched him as he put up his bag and carefully folded over his coat and jacket military-style into the empty seat between them, the outer shoulders touching in the back, leaving the inside exposed. In fact everything about him was groomed, he was encased in a smooth-fitting shirt and tie and the pants of an usher-stripe uniform, and he removed from his pocket a small round comb he used to stroke his temples, a pleased smile on his face. He was very young, she observed, just how young she couldn't exactly tell, though the uniform and the full flesh of his face made him look almost thirty-six.

She was uncomfortably aware of her own fifty-two years, but thought she might pass as attractive to him due to her very straight, well-fitted suit showing off her figure, which was, however, a bit too "mature."

"You're impeccably groomed," she remarked. "Do they teach you that in your academy?"

His smile broadened. "My parents are Haitian diplomats and I grew up in Europe, where I'd love to return someday," he began, and proceeded to give her a rundown of his military and educational history, which included a stint at Fort Leonard Wood in Missouri.

It was worse than a peanuts airline, it was a mini-pretzels and a sip-of-pop sort of airline, a roomy jet yet somehow reminiscent of a Greyhound bus with the lavatories constantly, noisily, occupied, and a big screen showing *Melanie*, a preadolescent fantasy with a decidedly lesbian tinge. He paid for liquor in his soft drink, and ordered a pair of earphones. She wavered but decided no on both the liquor and the earphones, then—captive audience that she was, practically locked into her seat—couldn't help but watch the decidedly exaggerated movie without them: Melanie's abusive vulgar parents, her crush on the beautiful femme schoolteacher ending in a childhood idyll of adoption by the perfect mother, the butch headmistress complete with whips and leather, forcing the fat boy to eat chocolate cake before the whole school until he puked, and then secretly eating cake herself. When the movie was over and the cadet was handing back the earphones, she winked at him, "It was better without them." In any case, with or without earphones, the movie had killed two and one-half hours, and they were about to land.

She wondered if he would ask for her phone number. She didn't really want him to, but on the other hand would be insulted if he didn't. They had established a cozy rapport in a remarkably short time.

The moment came. His eyes glazed over, an on-the-make look came over his full mouth, "So where do you live in Manhattan?"

"In the Village," she said.

"Oh, and how long have you lived there?" he said.

Her breezy gesture, "Oh, long," prompted his quick-mouthed response, "Too long."

"I guess so," she admitted. Suddenly she felt like a left-over wallflower. The moment of pickup had passed. She was too old, even for an older white mistress in the Village.

The plane was dropping altitude. Her ears began to hurt, and she could hardly hear the pilot about the landing, let alone her newfound companion. Soon he was helping her with her bag, he had found a way to finally lock the bottom halves of her garment bag that was neat and efficient and she remembered her first impression about his grooming.

She decided to put a good face on it. "It was wonderful traveling with you," she said, as she held out her hand. "Maybe we'll meet again sometime, you never know."

XMAS EVE IN FLORIDA

The way Lori told it, Aunt Dot and Lori's mother, Gwen, were sure to have a run-in when Gwen finally made it down to Florida herself to consider semiretirement. You see, Aunt Dot, who was seventy-seven and phobic, lived in a trailer park on Gwen's charity; but Gwen in her own retirement wanted to continue living in a house. But Aunt Dot was fixated on the trailer camp and wanted to stay put till the end of her days. Fur was going to fly, but in the meantime Lori was waiting through early winter for her mother to come down from Syracuse, New York, to enjoy the Florida sun.

Aunt Dot was difficult to live with, to say the least. There was no privacy, especially during phone calls. Aunt Dot thought all day about the crabmeat she was going to serve for supper; in the evening she watched *Wheel of Fortune* and waited for *Lucy* at nine, when she drank herself into a stupor as a way of falling asleep. (She ordered liquor by the case.) Sometimes glimpsing Lori writing or drawing she tried to imagine what it would have been like to have had a daughter of her own.

Lori tried to make herself useful around the trailer, and won her aunt over by doing a paint job. She signed up for an art class and tried to make herself scarce. She spent four days working on a Christmas present for Aunt Dot: a board/card game with poker chips. At least it would be a way to interact.

On Christmas Eve she hung up the stocking that her mother had sent, and set out the sugar cookies. Later that night they drove around the trailer camp to look at all the lights people had strung about their humble abodes. It was not exactly carols in the snow (this was Florida, remember), but people were standing around in small groups hooting and whistling. After all it was Christmas Eve.

OBITS

MYRNA GLICKMAN

Rozzie made only three friends when she went to college at sixteen, and Myrna Suzanne Glickman was one of them. Rozzie first met Myrna when they were freshmen taking a music-appreciation course together at the University of Chicago: Myrna was astonished when Rozzie refused to turn off the tape machine one Sabbath day in the listening room due to her Orthodox Jewish religious observance. (Myrna was from a Conservative Jewish background herself, and her parents, like Rozzie's, were refugees from Europe.) By the end of that semester Rozzie had stayed overnight in Myrna's dorm and later visited her in her hometown of Windsor, Ontario, where her mother ran around like a chicken without its head over a "tea ball" being out of its teapot, left on the table staining the Sabbath linen. Myrna's father was chinless, withdrawn, and absent most of the time. Rozzie realized she wasn't the only one from a neurotic Jewish family.

By the time Rozzie got to art school, she was a beatnik through and through, living on Clark Street (Chicago's Bowery), whereas Myrna remained straight and bourgeois as when Rozzie had first met her taking notes for Western Civ. 101. Nonetheless, Rozzie invited Myrna to her digs in a former settlement house and they spent a wild weekend careening around in a car with a bunch of guys who had come in with Rozzie's short-term boyfriend Marty, a handsome sailor. Myrna was shocked out of her mind by the whole experience.

Somehow they both ended up in New York where Rozzie became an organizer of the women's liberation movement. Rozzie recruited Myrna, and it stuck. Myrna was working at *Time* magazine, living in the far West Village on Hudson Street, and she was straight as ever. She got involved with Women in Media, and drifted into a West Village cell group of NY Radical Feminists. When this group planned a (successful) coup to overthrow the organizing principles of the founding Stanton-Anthony Brigade based in the East Village, of which Rozzie was a founding member, Rozzie resigned and never saw Myrna again. (It's possible she passed her in the street once or twice, but Rozzie could never be sure it was really Myrna for they didn't speak.)

It was not that Rozzie blamed Myrna for the coup—Myrna was always timid and had a follower's role in the supposedly leaderless group—but Rozzie knew Myrna was a satellite of the leader Leslie Modrell who had undone Rozzie and all her (unpaid) organizing that took over a year. (When Rozzie left the group it had five hundred members organized in cell groups all over the city; a year or two later she heard it was down to seven or so members.)

Some twenty years later, Rozzie received a call from Myrna Glickman. Myrna said she was doing well, that she was still working her straight job, that she now lived in a loft, and had gotten married at last the year before. Rozzie imagined a nice little copyeditor at *Time* making the plunge with longtime steady Myrna, and moving into her loft with her. Myrna remained in Rozzie's eyes the somewhat chinless freshman she had known. But when it was revealed that she was still orbiting Leslie Modrell, who had cost Rozzie her last group in the women's movement, Rozzie decided not to call Myrna back. Neither did Myrna call Rozzie again.

Two years passed. One day Rozzie got a call from a friend who had just spoken to Leslie Modrell. It was bad news about Myrna. It seemed that, contrary to Rozzie's fantasy, Myrna's marriage hadn't worked out at all well; she had married a Serb who abused her and wouldn't let her go out; she had lost her longstanding job as a researcher at *Time* for not being able to learn computers; she had eye trouble and had been acting strangely (such as holding her cards close to her chest at weekly poker games at Leslie's house); and she had taped two pairs of glasses together before her sister finally took her to an eye specialist who discovered … a brain tumor the size of a golf ball! No wonder she had been acting so strangely!

Myrna went into the hospital and was given the option of an operation with only a 50 percent chance of survival—and then she would probably be mentally impaired. Who could blame her for refusing to undergo the operation??

But the upshot of it was that Myrna had just died in the hospital at age fifty, tumor and all.

JEREMY SALZBURG

The Great Poet was dead. With the unlikely name of Jeremy Salzburg, he had entered the lives of thousands of people, many of them intimately, and helped to shape their lives. In cubicles all across the Big Apple, indeed America and the World, individuals recalled him, mostly with fondness, for he had been a warm friend and a supporter of the good in countless causes. But his excellent character was not all. He was truly a great man, but his oeuvre that he left behind was nothing short of astounding for the twentieth century: he was a Great Poet, influenced by Blake and Whitman and carrying on their tradition of epic poetry, at a time when all around him was aridity.

One of the people whom he so touched was Naomi Levine. For many long years she had loved him from a distance. She had read his work avidly from the age of sixteen and it was to his influence that she largely attributed her own coming out as a beatnik in the early sixties. She knew of his homosexuality but she secretly trusted that he was bisexual, as his cultivation of a female protégée, Jill Erikson, implied. (But this very protégée, so thin and fashionable and trendy, was what put her off and kept her at a distance. The protégée was at his side for twenty years, reading her own work with veritable orgasmic energy way beyond what she at first seemed capable of.)

Then Naomi met one of his male lovers, Hal Jackson, and even began going with him. The vicarious proximity to the Great Poet made her feel important. She was nourishing Hal, who in turn was a fallback for Jeremy when he needed to get out of his cramped circle for a bit and hide away for a few days in a West Village apartment. (Hal kept his apartment almost old-maidishly neat and clean, and he always had a genuine quilt on the bed. And he played an alto sax, something that came out of his thin frame as silver prayers.)

With her women friends from her consciousness-raising group she discussed the relation of the Great Poet to his mother, which Naomi thought guilty in the extreme. Jeremy, who was the only one living with his paranoid mother at the time, had signed commitment papers that locked her up for life and gave permission for a lobotomy. But maybe if he could play it again he would behave differently. Maybe at bar mitzvah age he had been just too young to know what to do, and now that he was older he may have learned more mature behavior. At least she hoped so.

Was it guilt over his mother that made him homosexual? Maybe he longed for a good Jewish wife but he had gone too far out for that to happen. But of course she shamed herself with such thoughts. Probably he was the bad boy he was reputed to be, homosexual to the core. The repugnance in the poem about his mother's dementia extended to her privates. And just look, for example, at the work of his close friend since the forties, Wallace Staples. A demonic inferno.

But still Naomi trusted in Jeremy's essential goodness and rightness of judgment. One had to rebel in the boring and straight fifties, and the rightness of his rebellion had been proven even more so in the following decades as the excesses of capitalism and the Kali Yuga had only stiffened.

Certainly *she* could never fit into the straight world. That's why she followed Jeremy's literary successes and all his changes—such as his initiation into Buddhism—so avidly. He was a map for her. And so she took yoga and ate basmati rice and continued to attend all his readings almost unconsciously, and to give his books to her friends. He shed a light she almost took for granted, he opened a little circle in which she could breathe.

In spite of this, she ended up in the hospital. And one of the elements of her madness was her love-hate relationship with Jeremy Salzburg, which was based on no real interaction between them. When she came out of the hospital, she determined to set the relationship on a real basis before it was too late. She was getting old and Jeremy was even older. How long was she going to follow him at a distance? Shouldn't he know that someone out there loved him? (But of course, thousands of people probably did.)

The old barrier, his protégée, was down, because Jill Erikson had moved out of New York City to run Jeremy's literary program—at a Buddhist ashram Jeremy had been instrumental in forming, which was growing bigger and richer and more prestigious all the time.

Somehow Naomi found a way to get his unlisted number. She left a message on his answering machine, that she wanted to meet him, that she was a friend of an old friend of his, Hal Jackson; and wouldn't you know, he called her back. They talked about Hal, who had gotten rich off his vegetarian restaurant, had married and divorced, leaving him with two little girls. Naomi told him she was fresh out of the mental hospital and Jeremy seemed interested. She invited him to lunch, at Hal's old restaurant, which was now taken over and gentrified, macrobiotic, and in their neighborhood (Jeremy lived only two blocks away from her); and he accepted.

The big day arrived, and Naomi and some of her girlfriends chose a secluded booth in the back of the restaurant where they could talk. She was very excited. She had told him to bring whom he liked and for her part she did not want the pressure of a private date. She felt strong in the company of her girlfriends, some of them young and strong dykes new to the movement who were glad to accompany her. She wore overalls, because that was how she most pictured him; but actually these days he was wearing a suit (upon the advice of his guru).

The time passed. Where was he? He was almost an hour late, when finally one of the girls buzzed: there he is. He came in with a young male companion, looking sallow and annoyed: he had had a problem with his toilet. He ordered only a bowl of soup and his companion, Bill, a carrot juice; Naomi was disappointed for she had been saving her skimpy disability money to treat him to a full-course luncheon. Evidently this luncheon did not mean as much to him as to her, that was for sure.

But, used to an audience on the Beats, he finally relaxed and waxed on about Dean Moriarty's last days. The women listened enthralled, though it was not precisely what they had come to hear.

Finally, Naomi mentioned that she had heard Yury Poliakoff, Jeremy's longtime lover, read his own poetry, and at this Jeremy sat up. He took advantage of the receptive and supportive audience of young females to go into his now-failed relationship with Poliakoff, who had been known to run off and marry a woman, but was now in bad mental shape and on neuroleptic drugs. Naomi said she had seen Poliakoff asking the audience to lend him a pair of glasses when he read, and going on about his recent trauma of police arrest which got him severely medicated on Haldol: "Did you ever try that stuff?? Whew!! You can't sleep!" And Naomi had.

From here Jeremy relaxed and opened up and actually seemed to enjoy the company of women. Before he left, he was nice enough to give Naomi and her foremost comrade the address and date of a party at his house. How did he know that this was precisely what Naomi needed most?

Naomi was cheered that her relationship with Jeremy had begun. But as luck would have it, the wrong day was written down (though the date was correct) and she and Anne arrived at a darkened apartment. They left a worried note. It was not until a few days later that they ran into Salzburg's young companion of the carrot juice, who glowed about a party the night before, held at a hall at NYU because there were just too many people for Salzburg's small apartment.

At his next poetry reading, Naomi tried to straighten the matter out. But Salzburg insisted that he couldn't have made the mistake. Sure enough, when Naomi checked back to the little slip of paper she had been carrying around to prove it wasn't *her* mistake, the date was correct but not the day and place. But she knew it hadn't been intentional. Much good that did her!

It was a year and a half before Naomi saw Salzburg again. By that time she had had a full relapse and yet another recovery. Salzburg had figured in her fantasies once again.

She was given a tip by a friend who was on a shoot at a café where one of Salzburg's male protégés was scheduled to sing that Salzburg had appeared to show his support. She went to the café and kept stealing peeks at Salzburg. When the concert was over (it was folkie) her tip-off person wanted to be introduced. She was embarrassed that

Salzburg did not immediately remember her until she mentioned her name. Then he was warm. He started giving her a rundown on Poliakoff, whom he said was now on lithium, living in an uptown SRO hotel. He asked her how she had been. "Oh, hanging in there," she said, which rang hollow when she remembered her relapse. She looked a lot better than she had the day she met him in her overalls, but she realized her mistake in trying to act normal: it had been precisely her hospital experience that interested him and distinguished her from just another student doing a paper on the Beats. Before he left, he embraced her so that she felt her braless breasts full against his chest. She fit together with him nicely and once again she wondered if he might be bisexual and interested in a younger woman to pep him up. But this time, instead of just Bill, he was accompanied by a small entourage of handsome young gay men, while she introduced only one young woman, the filmmaker; they had traded places. He seemed dignified but doddering and she imagined that he must be in his late seventies. She dreaded to think it would be the last time she saw him, and that's why she went to his next big poetry reading. There was standing room only and she saw him from behind a pillar, surrounded this time by a whole orchestra of handsome young men, not a woman among them. Approaching him through the mob of people seemed an impossibility, even if he could recall her, which she doubted.

Next she heard of his death—at only seventy(!)—it was in all the papers but she didn't think she ought to go to the memorials, it would only distance her from the few personal memories she had managed to glean before he died. She read that there were sixty people at his deathbed, like Solomon's warriors, but she hadn't been informed. She realized that even though he had introduced her to several people, she didn't know a single one of his friends to call, and Hal was long gone. Even the details of his death didn't come together in any sensible way: How could liver cancer give you a heart attack or a stroke? Hadn't the news of his terminal diagnosis of four to six months on liver cancer come out in the paper just the day before? Then maybe he reacted with a heart attack, or maybe he took some poison and then invited his closest friends to his deathbed in the manner of Socrates. If this was the case then his friends were all involved in a cover-up. There was no one to ask.

She wondered about his being disembodied. She felt nothing, not even a dream. But then why should he appear to her, when she had been excluded from his deathbed? But she was comforted by a little item in the paper within the week, that a deer had been found trying to crash the fence to the White House. Maybe he had entered that deer.

THE WAKE

The three Graces were the first ones at the funeral home in Pelham. (That they all three shared that first name in common was the cause of their acquaintanceship that had ripened over the years into friendship.) Grace Binion made haste to seek out the two bereaved sisters, Edith and Carole Ann, whose mother had died of a heart attack several days earlier, while Grace Kenardie (Mrs.) and Grace Pauling hung back exclaiming over the photo albums that showed Mrs. Hahn looking hale on a recent trip to the ruins of Palenque in the Yucatán.

The sons-in-law were everywhere and solicitous. It broke Grace Binion's heart when at last she found Edith, sobbing: "You know what Eric did, he made my mommy a casket."

But later shrieks were heard when the casket was opened for viewing behind a screen. Mrs. Hahn, to say the least, did not look like herself, but like something from a wax museum, with her hands carefully folded across her chest showing off some of her embroidery.

Grace Binion did not want another look; instead she busied herself writing some notes on her last memories of Mrs. Hahn, for use later when the gathering friends of the deceased shared their recollections and their pain. Others talked more extemporaneously, as the small family, Mrs. Hahn's husband and daughters, sat clasping hands and weeping. The death had been sudden and unexpected: Mrs. Hahn was only sixty-eight, and had just been scheduled for some hospital tests after complaining of angina pains. People spoke movingly, and everyone remembered her warmly, right down to her famous Dutch apple pie. She came alive in the retelling, and the grim body in the casket just within earshot seemed like a prop from a play.

Afterward there was a get-together at the house where several of the women had made a meal for the mourners. The daughters looked ravaged, and ate heartily. So did Grace Binion. It was a crusty pasta meal, and she came back for seconds. The house lacked only its hostess, who was all alone in a pine box back at the strange funeral home full of furniture without a kitchen or bedroom.

The three Graces got a ride back to Manhattan with Denise Jones, a young Black woman who had interned with Carole Ann in Philadelphia. This was where the trouble began for Grace Binion. All the food she had eaten, the choppiness of traffic, the closeness in the car—she was dreadfully nauseated. She pleaded for mercy and Denise was accommodating. She opened the windows to the cold winter air, and tried to drive more smoothly. Grace's stomach continued to churn. It was a long way to the topmost subway stop, and a long subway ride back. Could she make it without retching?

The two Graces conferred, and decided to get off at 110th Street just above their own stops (whereas Grace Binion lived downtown) to get some water and to walk Grace Binion briskly back and forth. If she was going to puke, best to do it now before she went on alone. But nothing happened. Her nausea eased slightly and she got back on the subway. "Tell me, will they bury her in the morning?"

"I have no idea what happens from here," replied Grace Pauling.

As the two Graces got off at 72nd Street, Grace Binion grimaced from between the closing doors, "Wish me luck. I'll probably throw up as soon as you leave."

And so she did. First the water came up. Then she got off and puked behind a post, the whole dinner, first once and then again. She was surprised in the cold night air that no one even looked at her in dismay.

I REMEMBER VALERIE

It was not that I admired her deed of shooting prominent pop artist Andy Warhol in the stomach over a squabble about some play she had presented for him to read and produce. Nor did I particularly value her book, the *SCUM Manifesto*: at the time I thought it had a dangerous leaning toward what would become matriarchalist theory in the women's movement, a glorification of women as they are in their oppressed state.

Frankly, I thought it was a big mistake to recognize Valerie as one of us, a women's liberationist, let alone to embrace her book as serious feminist theory. (I thought the initiative for this was coming from the media.) I'd also heard from Ti-Grace Atkinson that Valerie had threatened to throw acid into Ti-Grace's face when she went to visit her in prison. But I went to visit Valerie anyway because I'd heard she had moved just a block away from me since her release from Mattawan, an institution for the criminally insane. I wanted to see for myself and I was foolhardy in those days.

I found her in an apartment better than mine, ground floor, off the courtyard of a large brick building with white Doric columns in the front. The building was by far the nicest one on the block, Third Street between Avenues A and B, then next door to an Italian vegetable market. The room was simple and spare, the size of a small studio apartment, with a bed and a desk.

Valerie was slight, fair, aging, with a certain suspicious look in the eyes, and always with an overall poor-girl chic. She wore little white socks and her collar up, and she rolled her own cigarettes, carefully and with concentration, Big Top.

She grabbed my book from a narrow shelf above her bed and showed me where she had scored it all over. "I didn't like your book," she said, and began to quarrel with my theories. I defended myself as well as I could, and tried to change the subject. I did not see this as a meeting with a fellow theorist.

I gave her an underground paper I had brought, which had an article on how to call Europe free of charge. She was very grateful.

She waxed paranoid on the subject of the "Media Mafia" that was out to get her. I thought maybe it was true.

A young man appeared, who was very handsome in a weak sort of way. The effect of his looks wore off rather quickly when it appeared he was not too bright. But he seemed devoted to Valerie. I knew she was a lesbian, and interpreted this young fellow as someone she hung out with at Blimpie's, where she said she went at night. I figured it was all she could do to survive on the kind of welfare budget she was on.

After I returned home, I had a dream that she attacked me and hurt me. I decided not to go back.

FLASH FORWARD

Some time later, after I had moved to St. Mark's Place and was working as a muralist, I saw her in the street. She asked me for a quarter, and I saw that she was begging. She had lost her apartment, and presumably her welfare.

She asked for quite a few quarters after that, and I was sorry to see her turning into a mere panhandler in my eyes. One time I ran into her at a sandwich joint on St. Mark's main drag. She talked incoherently and the sound issued from deep within her throat, like someone with larynx trouble. She looked at me with hatred, and threatened me. I was deeply troubled. Were these the demons of killer psychosis, or did she just have a bad case of bronchial pneumonia and shouldn't be on the street? But I was too afraid of her to invite her into my sublet.

Later a friend of mine who ran a store on St. Mark's Place said that Valerie had approached him for shelter. She was covered with sores and wearing only a blanket to beg in. She had been out on the street approximately three months without shelter. Not long after that, she disappeared from the street entirely. She had been "picked up."

It was many years before I heard of her again. Then it was just an obituary stating that she had been found in a San Francisco hotel dead of lung disease.

Recently a movie came out titled *I Shot Andy Warhol.* Looks like the Media Mafia got Valerie after all. I didn't go to see it.

HARVEY

Elaine was leaving the Harm Reduction Center of the Lower East Side where she got regularly "pinned"—had acupuncture done on her ears for her drug problem—when she ran into Timothy Wallach, whom she had not seen in twenty years. They had been neighbors once, living on this very block between Avenues B and C when it was a drug trafficker's heaven. Now neither of them lived there.

He almost didn't recognize her at first, thinking that she was someone else he had known since. But then the name came back. "Elaine?" he apologized. "It's my short-term memory I have trouble with."

She surveyed him. He was still attractive, slim and bearded, though there was gray in his beard now. We should all have aged so well. "You used to be the super of 223. Where have you been? I haven't seen you in ages."

"Well, we moved out to Brooklyn for seven years, and then to Western Massachusetts. I'm a union carpenter now."

She noted the royal "we" and her glance fell to his ringed finger. "And what are you doing back in your old haunts?"

"Clem Whiteside and Angel Rodriguez—remember them?—invited me down here for a Fourth of July roof party to watch the fireworks from the East River. You get a good view from 223."

She almost invited herself to the party, then remembered that twenty years had passed and Tim was married. Instead she said, "In that building, I used to visit …"

"Harvey," he finished for her. "Everyone did. His kids are coming to the party. Do you remember Jade and Amber? They have kids of their own now."

"And Harvey and Sparrow? How are they? I lost touch with them. It's been a long time."

Tim gaped. "Don't you *know*? Harvey's been dead for eight years now, he died of a heart attack. He had been thrown out of 223 for about a year, he was trying to make it in Brooklyn. And Sparrow died three years ago, of AIDS."

"Oh, I'm sorry to hear that," Elaine mumbled. But she was pierced to the heart and wanted to cry. Harvey had been her dealer for way over ten years, back in the sixties and early seventies. Harvey, ugly as Sluggo, an integral part of Elaine's youth as a runaway from Long Island, the one who first showed her how to shoot up. And he had always been there when she needed someone, good for a toke and a long conversation; while she herself was good for a clean pillow slip with yellow roses. She remembered well how he would offer her a free Thai stick even after he was on methadone treatment for his heroin addiction and had long since stopped dealing.

His worn-out druggie wife Sparrow was continually running away on her old man and the kids. Harvey had asked Elaine to babysit, like everyone else in the neighborhood, but in the end he had to do it by himself. The kids went hungry and neglected and barefoot, on welfare, but Harvey loved them and they were sharp. And beautiful. Harvey himself was a certain kind of brilliant criminal mind, fascinating. A character. There was no one else like him, though he was surrounded by a group of fascinating characters. Like Sonny, who used to prance about showing off the neat jackets he had lifted. All of them lined up to shoot up, fashionably gaunt on H. Harvey had a big *H* on his loft door. Heroin Harvey.

Then Elaine's friend, the gorgeous Carol, fell for Harvey's Puerto Rican friend Hector in a big way, and married him. Hector was a beautiful dude. "You're a babe in the woods," he told Elaine on a walk through Tompkins Square Park with all the bongo drums going. But it was Hector who needed protection. With Carol's help he tried to kick, but some time after he had left the city to straighten out he went back to his old ways. He ended up jumping out the window to his death. Devastated, Carol moved to San Francisco, from where she used to send lilting letters, never forgetting to ask about Harvey and Sparrow. But

Elaine had cut the connection to Harvey, blaming him for Hector's death, Carol's ruined marriage, and her own long-term addiction that had destroyed her health.

She was afraid that Tim would notice her tears. She had been silent for some time. "Well, so much water under the bridge, ay?" she managed. "I guess I'll be running along. It was great bumping into you after all these years. Enjoy the party."

Then, over her shoulder, she added, "Take care." In the old days, she reflected, she would have said, "Take it easy."

SUICIDES I HAVE KNOWN

CATHY HANDLER

Cathy was intense. She was dogged about her painting but it was no good probably because she was trying too hard. She did figures from the model, and they tended to be contrived and harshly lit. But woe unto anyone who did not take them as seriously as she did! She labored over them long hours of overtime, and she was so serious as to be—at the age of twenty-one—formidable.

She looked good. She had dark curly hair, a short mop, and a dark brow—her mother was Irish and her father Jewish—and she missed beauty only by the prominent cast of her jaw. I assumed that she had slept around quite a bit before she started going steady with Stephan. I knew of one instance in particular, and I knew she had been a barmaid in Hyde Park, the University of Chicago turf—a multiracial oasis in the midst of the largely Black South Side of Chicago. So I just assumed.

It was the beginning of our friendship when she confided over lunch at the Art Institute of Chicago (where we were both students) that she had had a falling out with her closest friends, Carl and Diane Saulter. Cathy intimated that she was bisexual, but that Diane had thrown her out of the apartment when she found out about Cathy's involvement with Diane's husband Carl, as well as herself. At least this is what I made of her clues at the time: it was the sixties, long before gay liberation made such things open talk, at least in some quarters.

After this she had gone to Stephan, or he had come to her, I can't now remember which, and many months later they were still living together and talking of traveling together and even, eventually, marrying. Now Stephan had a harelip, but other than this he was a fine strapping figure of a man who was not ashamed of his disfigurement. (It came to seem his peculiar characteristic, so that one was shocked to see the same harelip on other faces.)

One day in school on the benches in front of the lockers Cathy and I had a very long talk that went on for hours. I was a compulsive talker then, once I got going, and I'm afraid I was all too compelling. We discussed feminism, art and art careers, the meaning of existence, everything. I thought we were getting close.

But the following week Cathy admitted that the talk had churned up a lot of trouble deep within her and she was disturbed. We only continued our talk.

Then it was Thanksgiving weekend, for which school closed early. On the day after Thanksgiving Stephan called me to ask if I had seen Cathy. She had disappeared on

Thanksgiving after a long talk with her father the night before. I made a few calls. No one had seen her. Stephan said she had not taken her purse with her.

Diane said Cathy was the type who would hitch a ride to Mexico with a quarter in her pocket. But the days went by and there was no word.

Finally we got the electrifying news that her mother had identified a bloated body in the morgue. Cathy had jumped off the Point in Hyde Park into the lake early that cold November morning some days after her Scorpio birthday, which I had seen her celebrate complete with candles on a chocolate cake. News from a biker with whom I got a ride indicated that her wrists had also been slit.

I was dumbfounded. I was young and it was the first death close to me. I couldn't imagine how she could have been so disturbed that she could cut her wrists and jump into icy water on a raw November morning. (Stephan said she had gotten up about 7:00 a.m. to go for a walk.) I felt guilty: Was it our talks that had done it? But she had also had a long talk with her father, the night before, and he had no inkling of what she was about to do. And she had slept with Stephan as usual.

I wrote poetry. Carl made a film. Diane went to a therapist. ("Couldn't she just have seen, on the way to the Point, say, a cat on the street, to remind her how beautiful life is?") A tiny print, a self-portrait, mounted in a large mat, in my opinion the best thing Cathy had ever done, was moved to a more prominent place in the Saulter living room. Her parents took the suicide badly, especially her father, an accountant, with whom she had been close. And her boyfriend Stephan was painting away on a streetscape, a good one, when he demurred on going to her small memorial—just wooden chairs lined up and no one in particular in charge. Two weeks later he threw out her clothes and books and paintings, and a beautiful blond student moved in, whom he eventually married. (But it was said, in his defense, that his mother too had almost married someone who committed suicide during the engagement. Maybe he was in flight from the recurring pattern.)

A small black-bordered announcement appeared on the desk of the receptionist at school. And that was it.

SHELDON KREM

I should have married that guy. Or at least had a deep affair with him. But just when I was on the verge of getting involved—he was the instructor in my creative writing workshop—my sister came to town and cautioned me against it as imprudent, perhaps because of the age difference (I was in my early twenties and he I believe was then close to forty). I veered away from our growing closeness without explanation, and he became less interested in my writing.

Sheldon was square jawed and stocky, with dark hair and dark plastic eye frames, Jewish, a shy smile, the whole impression something like a hipster jazz musician of the late fifties, a clean-cut hipster—and this was when he had done the writing that put him on the publishing map. I was a buxom Jewess with glasses like his and long frizzy hair, aggressive in some ways but shy.

When the workshop produced an anthology, I submitted a story in the first person about a hooker. It's possible they all believed this narrative was true of me but it was only partially true. In any case, Don Spanton and Michael Winther, who were acting as editors, threw out my story and substituted one of their own on the same subject. Only Sheldon was loyal enough to raise an objection— formerly he had been my champion—but the substitution went through anyway.

Early on, Sheldon had talked about publishing a short story of mine, "The Morgue Story," in the *Provincetown Review*, but that had been abandoned. Now all of them were surprised when I published on my own a book on radical feminism, which seemed quite successful. He had recognized my talent, and that I was on the verge of publication, but he could no longer be credited with discovering me.

The workshop ran its course and closed. I fell out of touch with my fellow participants, but the last thing I heard was that Sheldon was teaching in the famous U. of Iowa Creative Writing Program. I knew he lived near me in the East Village because I had once submitted a prophetic epic about race revolution under his door, to no response. He lived off Tenth Street near St. Mark's Church, on the better side of Second Avenue.

From time to time I passed him in the street: the first time I was wearing square-cut forties shorts, in light blue, which were flattering. But the second time, some ten years later, I was wearing a dingy postal-blue V-cut cardigan which was considerably shabbier, and revealed that I was down on my luck. As a matter of fact, I had moved to his block, Tenth Street, but on the other side of the tracks. He looked at me ruefully. We barely spoke, but the recognition was certain. He took in my whole situation at a glance.

It was long after I came out of the hospital that I heard he died. But something did not sit right. He was still young, and he had been teaching at Columbia. I remembered his early work about his stays in mental hospitals. But when I suggested it might be a suicide, this was dismissed. He had had a heart condition, I was told.

It was not until some years later that I met someone who knew the whole story. He had been alone, as always, in his tiny New York City apartment. He had left a suicide note. "I die with a smile on my lips." I tried, but couldn't, dismiss the association with a joke in my book, urging women to a "smile boycott."

YVONNE TREE

Before I ever met Yvonne Tree I met her in her work: square, straightforward compositions on the grotesque. I was a young art student then, and I had a Yashica 2¼ camera and I enjoyed composing on it. She had a strong influence on me, though I stopped short of getting into actual carnival grotesquerie as too sensationalistic. But the static posed quality of some of her frames affected my own photography—I am thinking now of her famous twin girls staring at the camera.

When I came to New York and began organizing women's liberation groups, we were to do publicity for a major piece in *The New York Times*. We were offered a choice of photographers and she was one of them. I was flattered to have such a great photographer assigned to us, and convinced the others that we should go for her. So we got her.

She was delicate boned, thin and pretty, if in a mousy sort of way. What I mean is she did not stand out as strong among the rest of us strapping girls. One night she accompanied us on an "action" to retrieve my pay from a withholding boss. (I was working as a waitress at McGregor's Garage on St. Mark's Place.) We ganged up on the boss and I threw a glass of water in his face. We got the pay. But Yvonne had stayed outside the whole time, quaking for possible damage to her expensive camera.

When the piece for the *Times* finally came out, the women were outraged at her photographs, which were of zombielike dykes all alone in a room. She had used one or two women from another group (who were not even typical) and distanced them in the space. I guess you could tell they were photos by Yvonne Tree.

I realized my poor judgment in swaying others in her favor when she apologized for the strangeness of the photographs, pleading that this was her "eye" and she was incapable of shooting a normal journalistic picture. I had rather thought she was doing this assignment for commercial reasons and that she would adapt her style accordingly, but I was wrong. Anyway, I believed her that she couldn't help it.

Later she destroyed a whole roll and only that which had been printed with the article on women's liberation remained with *The New York Times*. She, however, gave me as a casual gift one unused print that remained, ruined for any practical use by a large crease across the left corner. "You're not a beautiful girl," she said, "but somehow in this picture ..." And it was true, I looked stunning in the picture, a whole aura surrounded me; I was circled by other women who looked supplementary. I was wearing a long silver ring on the first finger of my right hand, my "Jupiter" finger—when I seldom wore a ring—and generally I read as the leader of the group.

In a taxicab once she had talked a little about the breakup of her long marriage—she seemed to be about forty at the time—to a young guy who had launched her on her career as one of the few significant female artists of that era. Otherwise I had no clue that she was deeply depressed, other than her tearing up the roll of women's lib shots which were neither fish nor fowl—neither her usual strong grotesques, nor a good journalistic visual account of what was developing in women's liberation.

Anyhow, a month and a half later we heard a shocking story: her body had been found in the bathtub, drained of blood. She had apparently chosen to go by cutting her wrists and then hastening the flow of blood by letting it seep into warm water. It all sounded gruesome. I had had no idea she was in such a desperate state.

I held on to the picture as exceedingly valuable. I hid it in some newspapers behind an old trunk, and then later decided to put it in a cardboard roll in another place I had. When I came out of the hospital, I had no money, so I called a curator at the Museum of Modern Art to see if they might not want to buy the picture, one of her last good shots. But they were content to settle for the *New York Times* shots, in which I had (gratefully) not been included. In any case, I checked for the roll of cardboard, and it had been thrown out in my absence.

DANNY

Danny was my brother, not a year apart from me in age
(we celebrated our birthdays in the same week in January:
his was January 13, 1944, and mine was January 7, 1945)
so that we were almost like twins. But Danny was a beautiful angelic-looking blond with an aura, whereas I was a
moody Spanish-looking little girl with sturdy knees and
olive skin and my dark hair in braids wrapped on top of
my head, both of us frequently dressed in crinkly clean
cotton jumpsuits. The first word out of my mouth was
"Danny," presumably a yell of glee when we went to
explore our new house in St. Louis where we had moved
from Kansas City. I remember him beheading a baby doll
in Kansas City, to see how the eyes blinked and what was
inside her (stuffing) and the finding of a brown egg laid by
a chicken in the backyard. But most of my memories of
play were from the house in St. Louis, a small stone house
with a backyard which we all loved and felt possessive
about—especially when we found large life-size graffiti on

the walls of our canvas sukkah, including a few penises. Inside the house we slid down the "chute," a painted stairway leading to the kitchen which was sealed off to throw laundry down to my mother at the bottom—we loved to tumble down the stairs amidst the slightly smelly laundry especially when she wasn't home. We laughed at the babysitters who hid under the beds during a thunderstorm, in which we ran to the windows and exulted in the wind, rain, and lightning.

We licked the bowls when my mother made cakes, and went to the candy store pretty often, where there was a wealth of penny candy of all sorts—including wax teeth, moustaches and lips, long sheets of "buttons" in pretty rows of pastels, "kits" of tiny packaged squares of taffy that came in waxed paper wrappers of five per flavor, chocolate, strawberry, or banana. We had "candy collections" in our rooms, and we would come out at night to trade and play with them. There was a brouhaha that we ate my sister's candy, and in general we excluded her from our team until she had a dream that we were running away and leaving her far behind. She became a pet of my parents who were always worried about her frailty, relative to our sturdiness. When I was about four my brother got nickel candy, Milk Duds in a small carton, which my mother said was for recess in school. I wondered what "recess" meant and what "school" could be like.

I always seemed to share a room with my sister, especially in later years, while my brother was across the hall.

One time after bedtime I remember playing with his (circumcised) genitals, which were sweet and hairless and innocent—making them dance.

After I joined him in school, we had virtually identical educations. Even the class difference didn't matter much, as he had a large class of twenty or so children whereas my class was only five or six—so we frequently doubled up. It was a small school, an Orthodox Jewish academy on its first legs in an indifferent environment, and it had many funding and other difficulties, so we ended up with practically private tutoring. We learned Bible in Hebrew every day till noon, and then, to satisfy state requirements, we did the three R's with mostly retired non-Jewish teachers. My brother and I were excellent at English and we won all the spelling bees. We were good at history too, but fell down in math (though I was worse than he was, just as I was a little bit better in English). In seventh and eighth grade we won the favor of a schoolmarm, ca. World War I, named Viola Mae Bascom, and we became stars. This was interrupted by my going off to stay with relatives in Detroit (I thought it would help the religious conflicts I was having) where I lost my heady glow and came back so poor in decimals that I was almost unable to graduate eighth grade.

Did I say that my brother's favorite colors were bright blue and orange? Or that he had a concentration of planets in the ninth house of higher education?

Did I say that my brother was becoming increasingly "antisocial"? He swore he would never marry (so did I).

From about the age of seven or eight our tight partnership had split and he stopped speaking to me, or only rarely. I was heartbroken for I worshipped him. But there was nothing to be done and no explanation. Our parents fought, and the heavy-duty religious observance they imposed on us contributed to our neuroses. Both of us needed glasses and were turning chubby and were stunted in growth.

My brother delivered newspapers and when he was driven off that by the Irish clans on the block—who used to chase us around the porch with rubber knives accusing us of killing Christ—he took to selling combs in the Turkish baths. He had a big collection of comic books he used to trade and read, whereas I read fairy tales. My interest in stray animals increased the less hospitable toward them my mother became ("I have enough animals of my own to take care of"). There was a bad incident with some little ducks that died of the cold in the hall because my mother didn't want them in the house proper. Meanwhile my brother became interested in shooting his BB gun in the backyard. One day I found him torturing some little stray kittens of mine by sticking a wooden twig into their throats and twirling them around and around on it.

He hated girls, of which there were quite a few in his class who made a point of being attractive, Marcias and Sheilas who wore fifties sweater sets and poodle skirts and had hankies all wrapped up in their soft nail-polished hands. He wouldn't play spin the bottle or other necking games which excited me even from a distance. And then there was dancing, which my father forbade on religious grounds. (Those were the days of Dick Clark and the jitterbug.)

My brother resolved all this by going to yeshiva in Cleveland, Ohio, and after a few months of public school, I followed into the girls' division of the yeshiva, which was a makeshift high school operating with only sixteen students school-wide. I was soon miserable in my boarding school, and my brother did not make a much better adjustment to yeshiva.

My mother insisted we call each other at least once a month but it was always painful. We had little to talk about and I soon embarrassed him with a reputation for being boy crazy. My childhood sweetheart, David Zbar—later killed by a landmine in Israel where he had married a Sephardic woman after divorcing a gentile wife—ended up at Danny's yeshiva, from where he called me. We had quite a flirtation going on, but Danny was sternly disapproving: "He's a joker, he smokes and likes girls, he draws instead of learning." The more he talked about him the better I liked him. Then there was the time he lectured me about peeping through the holes of the *m'chitza* (curtain between men and women in prayer) on Yom Kippur, when actually I had been fasting and even (optional religious observance) not speaking for twenty-four hours. On certain holidays we girls went out to stay with the families of the rabbis in the yeshiva. I remember one time in particular when my brother was called for to visit me at his rebbe's and he wouldn't come. No explanation. I was thoroughly embarrassed.

But as we got closer to college age, my brother softened. He wanted to go to college, with virtually no encouragement from any quarter. I wanted to go too. I had been sneaking in college texts on English literature, and playing a run-down old record player with *A Selection from the Classics* that my mother gave me: pretty turgid stuff, Dvořák, Smetana, Grieg, Richard Strauss's *Death and Transfiguration*. I bolted my door, which was against the rules, and spent hours alone, listening, reading, writing, and dreaming. Here is one memory of Danny which was positive: I had somehow discovered Dostoevsky's *Crime and Punishment* which I read through in one sitting of a couple of days, going without meals or breaks. I was very much moved by the book and I called my brother as the only one I could talk to about it. He was receptive and we had a long talk about it for several hours. I was grateful.

For about one year in there, when we started college together (I had finished high school in three years), he was sociable. Perhaps he was grateful that he had someone to share his college experience with. We were both on loans, with no family encouragement. My brother did the almost crippling thing of continuing yeshiva late at night even while carrying a full load at college. He had his time scheduled down to five-minute periods, and his schedules were awful to see. He however set a good example of discipline for me: he had a briefcase and he used bright-yellow study primers which were all the rage then: synopses of plays, how to scan exam material, and so on. I was impressed with his seriousness about studying.

By our sophomore year, we had had another falling out. I was no longer observant, and one Sabbath when our parents were away he beat me for breaking the Jewish law. It was over some trifle I can't even remember now. But he never spoke to me again. The irony was that he would follow me soon enough into the secular world.

I saw him one more time. It was the beginning of our sophomore year, and I had already moved into my own apartment. My contact with my parents was minimal. I had registered for philosophy and I showed up there only to see my brother, the only other person in the room besides the instructor. I was embarrassed and transferred out.

Sometimes I passed him on campus. He did not say hello.

I did not see him for the twelve years thereafter until his death. I heard distant reports of him from my sisters, with whom I stayed in contact. That he left home. That he was in heavy-duty therapy. That he was majoring in classics, that he was studying five languages, Greek, Latin, German, Russian, and Chinese, that he was in graduate school at a Jesuit college, St. Louis University, and finally that he was teaching at the University of Missouri. It was said that he was dating "shiksas" and that he had a taste for sports car racing (presumably gambling). As he lost touch with my mother's Orthodox Jewish relatives, he began to cultivate my father's clan in Kansas City, who were more relaxed about religious observance (traditionalist at best) and just more relaxed in general—less European neurotic.

Pictures from this time showed him stocky, short haired with heavy glasses, and generally unattractive. He looked like he was medicated, with swollen fingers.

By this time the sixties were over, and it was time for the New Age. I myself was on the yoga path trying out every kind of Buddhism except Zen, for which I had a peculiar distaste. (Maybe I just didn't care for Alan Watts and the earlier popularization of Japanese Zen in the West, dating to the rise of the Beats in the late fifties. Anyway, Zen was undergoing a New Age revival.)

Then I heard that my brother had given up all his possessions and committed his life to a Zen center in upstate New York. Ithaca: a college town, leafy, quiet. I remember finding it amazing how similar our paths had been, even with no contact for over a decade. But as I noted, Zen was the only Buddhist path I had not investigated directly among a myriad that were opening up in the States, so our paths did not cross.

Two and one-half years later I was in my old blue-terrycloth robe at an odd hour when an acquaintance of my sister's made her way to Avenue B in the then still notorious "Alphabet City" in the East Village of Manhattan to bring me the shocking news that my brother had died, age thirty-one, in a car crash. She knew little more—I was in tears that I would never now be able to resolve our nonrelationship—but urged me to go to St. Louis, where my parents still lived, for the funeral. Despite my great distance from the family and even more so from my brother who was in contact with none of us, his sudden death was a clarion call. I knew my life would never be the same again.

Short of a mysteriously torn-up, illegible letter I had received when I was in art school in Chicago, my absolutely last contact with Danny had been by phone shortly before the occasion of the bar mitzvah of the baby of the family, for whom we all had a soft spot. But Danny was stoic in not breaking down even at my urging (black sheep that I was) to see the family again; and I admired this.

It took me over twenty-four hours to dig out of my father the bitter truth that the body had a bullet hole in the chest. By that time undertakers with shiny car and coffin were all over the front lawn and I was banging my fists against the stone wall of the hearth in the den of that twostory suburban house which I and my almost-twin had lived in but rarely and visited only between long stays in boarding school.

I remember the dangling receiver after my father, I believe at my urging, called the roshi at the Zen Center in Ithaca. There were recriminations, particularly about my brother having signed away all his property for life. My father was cynical about the whole thing.

Apparently Danny had taken almost all his money, about $3,000, out of the bank in preparation for the car trip to an Indian reservation outside of Taos, New Mexico; but though he had been gone only a week, the money was not found on him. Police corruption was suspected rather than highway robbery. But I suspected everything and everyone.

I rushed out of the house before the funeral, shrieking, "Can't you feel it? He's not in that coffin. He must be at the Zen funeral in Ithaca." And so I flew to Ithaca to investigate further, getting tipsy on the way.

I was met at the airport by a balded young acolyte in saffron robes, who took me to a house he lived in with other male students at the Zen Center. (The one female was a beautiful young woman named Margaret Lee, who took me under her wing though she was considerably younger than I was.) The young man was a former roommate of my brother, but he had little to offer about my brother's last years, as indeed, I found out, no one had. Danny had remained a loner even in this communal setting.

The "funeral" was at the main center, just meditation and chanting every day for a week with a more recent picture of my brother on the mantle: he was bearded and beginning to bald, but he looked healthier than in the last photo I had seen. The close contact I had had with my father so recently made me view through his eyes the tall gilded Buddhas lining the hall to the meditation center as so much idol worship.

Eventually I stayed in my brother's former apartment, which was meticulously neat and orderly, with a large collection of ginseng plants growing in jars all over the kitchen. I went through his books and his clothes, most of them in fine shape, and I quarreled with the Zen Center even about what was left in his bank account ($300, which they kept in the end). Then I called home preparing to ship his stuff, but my father called me a "ghoul" over the telephone and proceeded to fully enlighten me that it had been a suicide after all—in addition to his brown Buddhist robes and ginseng, the police had turned over a small meditation diary which had the date of death circled as "Final Ceremony," preceded by some other ceremonies, including money-burning ceremonies.

In other words, he had purposely chosen a secluded spot on an Indian Reservation that he knew of and meditated himself into the suicide, in which he shot himself at close range with his own gun. He had a real estate license, and, according to the roshi, he had once handled real estate for the Zen Center, checking out land very close to where he went to die. That he took a gun with him I knew because I saw with my own eyes a penciled note he left on the kitchen table with preparations scratched off, including a gun.

I gave most of his clothes and effects to the childless old couple who lived below him, who seemed to relate to him as a son they'd never had. They told me that before he left he had paced the floor nervously for several days; that he had been doing zazen on his mat for about nine hours a day; that he'd gotten into a quarrel over religion with a Jehovah's Witness on his shift as a night watchman. (I found evidence among his effects that he was job hunting unsuccessfully—an application to the University of Texas at Austin indicated he wanted to get out of New York State altogether.) I sent his *t'filin* home to my father, and a picture of his rebbe from yeshiva days. (Other than a photo of the youngest brother whose bar mitzvah he had declined to attend, there was nothing to indicate he was from a large bourgeois family in the Midwest.)

On my last day there someone appeared who seemed to have some information, but as he was arriving from another state, I later tended to doubt his story. He said that "Dan" had been chosen to prepare a meditation for the students but had been criticized for being argumentative in a Talmudical way antithetical to the Zen Path; and taking this to heart he had resigned from the center and hadn't been seen around for a period of about three months prior to his death trip. This was the first time I had heard about this from anyone, and in later years of paranoia I suspected this strange last-minute arrival on the scene was a government agent.

I went back to New York with more questions than answers, to a job in a redneck microfilm factory. I suspected that there had been no death diary, or why would my father have waited so long to tell me in order to convince me to drop my investigation? Or in later years, I wondered why my sister would refuse to show me the diary along with the autopsy and other death certificates. I thought that maybe it had been a murder by a former drug connection getting even on a debt. Or maybe it had been my own political limelight that had brought the heat down on him as a warning to me, hence the "government agent" theory.

I spent some years trying to find Danny in the spiritual realm, but I was told by more than one medium that his violent death had shattered his ethereal body so he couldn't be reached.

In the end, theories about his death, whether murder or suicide, afterlife or no, contributed to my own growing madness—which led to my hospitalization, medication, and a shattering nervous breakdown.

DEATH OF A REVOLUTIONARY

When Shulamith Firestone's body was found late last August, in her studio apartment on the fifth floor of a tenement walkup on East Tenth Street, she had been dead for some days. She was sixty-seven, and she had battled schizophrenia for decades, surviving on public assistance. There was no food in the apartment, and one theory is that Firestone starved, though no autopsy was conducted, by preference of her Orthodox Jewish family. Such a solitary demise would have been unimaginable to anyone who knew Firestone in the late 1960s, when she was at the epicenter of the radical-feminist movement, surrounded by some of the same women who, a month after her death, gathered in St. Mark's Church In-the-Bowery, to pay their respects.

The memorial service verged on radical-feminist revival. Women distributed flyers on consciousness-raising, and displayed copies of texts published by the Redstockings, a New York group that Firestone cofounded.

The WBAI radio host Fran Luck called for the Tenth Street studio to be named the Shulamith Firestone Memorial Apartment, and rented "in perpetuity" to "an older and meaningful feminist." Kathie Sarachild, who had pioneered consciousness-raising and coined the slogan "Sisterhood Is Powerful," in 1968, proposed convening a Shulamith Firestone Women's Liberation Memorial Conference on What Is to Be Done. After several calls from the dais to "seize the moment" and "keep it going," a dozen women decamped to an organizing meeting at Sarachild's apartment.

Midway through the service, the feminist author Kate Millett, now seventy-eight, approached the dais, bearing a copy of *Airless Spaces* (1998), the only book that Firestone published after her landmark manifesto, *The Dialectic of Sex: The Case for Feminist Revolution*, which came out in 1970. Millett read from a chapter entitled "Emotional Paralysis," in which Firestone wrote of herself in the third person:

> She could not read. She could not write. ... She sometimes recognized on the faces of others joy and ambition and other emotions she could recall having had once, long ago. But her life was ruined, and she had no salvage plan.

Clearly, something terrible had happened to Firestone, but it was not her despair alone that led Millett to choose this passage. When she finished reading, she said, "I think we should remember Shulie, because we are in the same place now." It was hard to say which moment the mourners were there to mark: the passing of Firestone or that of a whole generation of feminists who had been unable to thrive in the world they had done so much to create.

* * *

In the late 1960s, Firestone and a small cadre of her "sisters" were at the radical edge of a movement that profoundly changed American society. At the time, women held almost no major elected positions, nearly every prestigious profession was a male preserve, home-making was women's highest calling, abortion was virtually illegal, and rape was a stigma to be borne in silence. Feminism had been in the doldrums ever since the first wave of the American women's movement won the vote, in 1920, and lost the struggle for greater emancipation. Feminist energy was first co-opted by Jazz Age consumerism, then buried in decades of economic depression and war, until the dissatisfactions of postwar women, famously described by Betty Friedan in *The Feminine Mystique* (1963), gave rise to a "second wave" of feminism. The radical feminists emerged alongside a more moderate women's movement, forged by such groups as the National Organization for Women, founded in 1966 by Friedan, Aileen Hernandez, and others, and championed by such publications as *Ms.*, founded in 1972 by Gloria Steinem and Letty Cottin Pogrebin. That movement sought, as NOW's statement of purpose put it, "to bring women into full participation in the mainstream of American society," largely by means of equal pay and equal representation. The radical feminists, by contrast, wanted to reconceive public life and private life entirely.

Few were as radical, or as audacious, as Shulamith Firestone. Just over five feet tall, with a mane of black hair down to her waist, and piercing dark eyes behind Yoko Ono glasses, Firestone was referred to within the movement as "the firebrand" and "the fireball." "She was a flame, incandescent," Ann Snitow, the director of the gender-studies program at the New School and a member of the early radical cadre, told me. "It was thrilling to be in her company."

Firestone was best known for her writing. *Notes from the First Year*, a periodical she founded in 1968 (followed, in 1970 and 1971, by the *Second Year* and the *Third Year*), generated the fundamental discourse of radical feminism, introducing such concepts as "the personal is political" and "the myth of the vaginal orgasm." Most of all, Firestone is remembered for *The Dialectic of Sex*, a book that she wrote in a fervor, in a matter of months.

In some two hundred pages, *Dialectic* reinterpreted Marx, Engels, and Freud to make a case that a "sexual class system" ran deeper than any other social or economic divide. The traditional family structure, Firestone argued, was at the core of women's oppression. "Unless revolution uproots the basic social organization, the biological family—the vinculum through which the psychology of power can always be smuggled—the tapeworm of exploitation will never be annihilated," Firestone wrote. She elaborated, with characteristic bluntness: "*Pregnancy is barbaric*"; childbirth is "like shitting a pumpkin"; and childhood is "a supervised nightmare." She understood that such statements were unlikely to be welcomed—especially, perhaps, by other women. "This is painful," she warned on the book's first page, because "no matter how many levels of consciousness one reaches, the problem always goes deeper." She went on:

> Feminists have to question, not just all of *Western* culture, but the organization of culture itself, and further, even the very organization of nature. Many women give up in despair: if *that's* how deep it goes they don't want to know.

But going to the roots of inequality, Firestone believed, was what set radical feminism apart from the mainstream movement: "The end goal of feminist revolution must be, unlike that of the first feminist movement, not just the elimination of male *privilege* but of the sex *distinction* itself: genital difference between human beings would no longer matter culturally."

In one of the book's later chapters, Firestone floated a "sketchy" futuristic notion that she intended only "to stimulate thinking in fresh areas rather than to dictate the action." She envisioned a world in which women might be liberated by artificial reproduction outside the womb; in which collectives took the place of families; and in which children were granted "the right of immediate transfer" from abusive adults. Predictably, the proposal stimulated more outrage than fresh thought, though many of Firestone's ideas—children's rights, an end to "male" work and traditional marriage, and social relations altered through a "cybernetic" computer revolution—have proved prescient.

Dialectic was both lauded and excoriated, often in the same review; the *Times* called its author "brilliant" and "preposterous." It was ridiculed on talk shows as it climbed the bestseller list, and was cast as "the little red book for women" while it was changing worldviews in un-red female America. Millett, whose book *Sexual Politics* appeared the same year as *Dialectic*, told me, "I was taking on the obvious male chauvinists. Shulie was taking on the whole ball of wax. What she was doing was much more dangerous."

Firestone was equally important to women's liberation as an organizer. She launched the first major radical-feminist groups in the country, and played a key role in conceiving the movement's theoretical positions and organizational structures, and in reconnecting it to a lost history.

And she did this in just three years. Jo Freeman, a feminist writer and activist who worked with Firestone from the beginning, said at the memorial, "When I think back on Shulie's contribution to the movement, I think of her as a shooting star. She flashed brightly across the midnight sky, and then she disappeared."

* * *

Over Labor Day weekend in 1967, a coalition of leftist groups involved in the battles over civil rights and the Vietnam War convened the National Conference for New Politics, in Chicago. Two thousand young activists attended, including Firestone, who was then twenty-two. She was living in a gang-ridden neighborhood on the North Side of Chicago, working as a mail sorter at the post office and studying figurative painting at the School of the Art Institute of Chicago. She had come to Chicago from St. Louis, three years earlier, and her political experience was limited to a stint protesting racial policies at a St. Louis bank and a dalliance with the Catholic Worker movement. Yet, at the conference, she noticed immediately that a crucial topic had been left off the agenda: the secondary status of women. It was a common omission; the New Left was pervaded by a machoism typified by Stokely Carmichael's quip that "the only position for women" in the Student Nonviolent Coordinating Committee "is prone." It was then that Firestone met Jo Freeman, who shared her dismay, and they drafted a resolution calling for equitable marital and property laws, "complete control by women of their own bodies," and a 51 percent representation of women on the conference floor.

The chairman skipped over it. "They laughed at us," Freeman recalled. "The chair said, 'Move on, little girl. We have more important issues to talk about here than women's problems.' And then he reached out and literally patted Shulie on the head." Soon afterward, Firestone and Freeman convened Westside, the first radical-feminist group in Chicago. Yet many of the women in Westside, and its successor, the Chicago Women's Liberation Union, thought that the concerns of the male-dominated New Left should take priority. Naomi Weisstein, then a young neuroscientist at the University of Chicago, recalled, "The first thing the Chicago Women's Liberation Union did was vote to give half our money to the Black Panthers." Firestone, who had no interest in what she called "Ladies' Auxiliaries of the Left," united a faction that called itself, simply, the feminists.

A few months before the New Politics conference, some film students in Chicago had chosen Firestone to be the subject of a project on the Now Generation. Their gemlike documentary, *Shulie*, chronicling her life as an aspiring painter, captures her ardency. "I just keep thinking, Well, I'm twenty-two, what have I done?" she tells one of the directors, Jerry Blumenthal. "I want to do something. Instead of beauty and power occasionally, I want to achieve a world where it's there all the time, in every word and every brushstroke, and not just now and then."

* * *

That intensity emerged in Firestone early, and it was a source of antagonism within her family. She was the second child and the oldest daughter of six children—three girls and three boys—born to Kate Weiss, a German Jew who had fled the Holocaust (she came from a long line of Orthodox scholars, rabbis, and cantors), and Sol Firestone, a traveling salesman from an assimilated Jewish family in Brooklyn, who served in the army during the Second World War. In 1945, while Kate nursed the newborn Shulamith, Sol's unit marched into the liberated Bergen-Belsen concentration camp. As a teenager, Sol, studying on his own, had become Orthodox. With a convert's zeal, he controlled his younger siblings and, later, his children—especially his oldest daughter. As Tirzah Firestone, the youngest of the three girls, recalled, "My father threw his rage at Shulie."

Laya Firestone Seghi, the second daughter and the family peacemaker, who is now a psychotherapist, remembered an ugly fight when Shulamith was sixteen. Father and daughter grappled on the stairs, with Sol shouting, "I'll kill you!" and Shulamith yelling back, "I'll kill you first!" Firestone's younger brother Ezra suspected that the animosity derived from a deep commonality. "He wouldn't bend, and she wouldn't bend," Ezra said. "They were both very brilliant and very, very opinionated." Kate did not intervene. "My mother had this completely passive view of femininity that was governed by what she regarded as 'what Jewish women do,'" Tirzah said. Shulamith endlessly questioned her parents' tenets. When she asked Sol why she had to make her brother's bed, he told her, "Because you're a girl."

In the Firestone home, a girl who did not follow the rules was destined to be cast out. Laya violated the Sabbath once, by reading a book in bed with a flashlight, when she was seventeen, and was banished from the house. Tirzah married a devout Christian and was formally disowned. (Later, she embraced Jewish Renewal, a mystical approach to Judaism that champions feminine spirituality, and became a Renewal rabbi, earning further paternal opprobrium.)

Shulamith's younger brothers, Ezra and Nechemia, remained strictly Orthodox; Ezra later studied to be a rabbi, and Nechemia became a West Bank settler. Only the oldest son, Daniel, violated his father's wishes: instead of continuing his yeshiva education, he studied classics and philosophy at Washington University in St. Louis. Shulamith skipped a year of high school to join him there. Born less than twelve months apart, she and Daniel had been inseparable as children, "almost like twins," she wrote in *Airless Spaces*. But she added:

By our sophomore year ... I was no longer observant, and one Sabbath when our parents were away he beat me for breaking the Jewish law. It was over some trifle I can't even remember now. But he never spoke to me again.

"Marx was onto something more profound than he knew," Firestone wrote in *Dialectic*, "when he observed that the family contained within itself in embryo all the antagonisms that later develop on a wide scale within the society and the state." For her, the only family tie that proved sustaining was the one between sisters, in particular the one between her and Laya, who became, as Laya herself said, "Shulie's prime support system." They roomed together in Chicago, and, later, Laya served reluctantly as Shulamith's representative and mediator in movement disputes. "Shulie recognized the unfairness of it," Laya said. "She'd say, 'It's not right for me to make you into the wife.' But, at the same time, she needed it."

* * *

In October 1967, Firestone told the Westside group that she was moving to New York. "I assumed that she was going to advance her art," Freeman said. Several of Firestone's art-student friends told me that she was also fleeing a physically abusive boyfriend. In an unpublished roman à clef, which Firestone worked on during the decades before her death, she recalled his repeated beatings; one time, he hit her so hard that he knocked a tooth out of place. "I think she was afraid he was going to kill her," Andrew Klein, a close friend of Firestone's at the time, told me. The fear wasn't something that she shared with other feminists. The only "sister" she told was Laya.

In New York, Firestone settled in the East Village—then a declining neighborhood of Eastern European immigrants, which had become an outpost for both the drug trade and the counterculture. She took a one-room apartment on East Second Street, which she kept as an art studio when she found the place on Tenth Street. She worked as a cocktail waitress to support herself, and drew and painted in every spare moment. She made dark expressionist portraits of family members and also of solitary anonymous women and nineteenth-century radicals, including the abolitionist leader Frederick Douglass and the feminist writer Margaret Fuller.

Soon after she arrived, Firestone and Pam Allen, a civil rights activist she had met in Chicago, recruited half a dozen young women from civil rights and antiwar groups, and cofounded New York Radical Women, the first group of its kind in the city. They met weekly in the women's apartments or in a borrowed office on the Lower East Side. "That women would choose to get together to talk about their lives without any males present was radical," Allen says. "It freaked people out." Women who attended those early meetings describe a time of "euphoria," an "explosion of ideas," and a kind of "falling in love." In a letter to Laya, dated February 3, 1968, Firestone wrote, "I think we're really onto something new & good, that is, radical feminism, and if we don't get fucked up, we'll take a decidedly different direction."

Firestone was a catalytic force. "She already had the arguments, already had a plan," Colette Price, an early member of the group, told me. "To us she was the American Simone de Beauvoir." Carol Giardina, who went on to cofound Gainesville Women's Liberation, in Florida, the first such group in the South, said that Firestone knew "that groups have to have an organizing structure and principles ... or else you are just higgledy-piggledy all over the place." Yet hierarchy was anathema to many feminists, who saw leadership as oppressive and male, and sisterhood as a community of equals. Firestone ran afoul of this egalitarianism. She was impatient with "scut work," her former comrades recall; she "refused to collate," and "wouldn't type." The author and former *Ms.* editor Robin Morgan still sounds annoyed when she talks about the time that a few of the women decided to clean a meeting space, and Firestone said, "I'm an intellectual— I don't sweep floors." On one occasion, after Firestone had spoken at length, a woman chastised her for having "male hormones." Firestone pointed to her breasts and said, "But look at these!"

The sisterhood was no more welcoming to feminist "mothers." But Firestone, who had extensively researched feminism's first wave and had dedicated *Dialectic* to Simone de Beauvoir, believed that the new movement needed to know its historical progenitors and precedents to thrive. In the summer of 1968, Firestone was in Paris with Anne Koedt, a member of the New York group, and tried to deliver a copy of *Notes from the First Year* to Beauvoir. "Went to see S de B. on Sat.," Firestone wrote to Laya. "She wasn't home & a horrible woman concierge barked at us that we need an appointment." They left the journal and a message, but Beauvoir was away for the summer.

In January 1969, on a trip to Washington, DC, Firestone and a couple of other women knocked on the door of Alice Paul, who had written the original Equal Rights Amendment, in 1921, and who was then in her eighties. She ushered them into a dark parlor, where old National Woman's Party literature was spread out on the tabletops. "She was very suspicious of us," Barbara Mehrhof, one of the visitors, recalled. Paul pointed to a wall of framed oil portraits of formidable-looking women—all suffragist leaders—and demanded that they identify them. "We didn't have any idea," Mehrhof said. "Which was just emblematic of the whole problem: How can we pass the torch when we don't even know who we are?"

The women were in Washington to attend the New Left's Counter-Inaugural to Richard Nixon's first inauguration. Late in the protest, under a large tent set up near the Washington Monument, the antiwar leader Dave Dellinger, serving as master of ceremonies, announced, "The women have asked all the men to leave the stage." They hadn't, but his words gave a nasty impression, made worse by the sight of a paraplegic Vietnam veteran being carried off to make way for the "women's libbers." Marilyn Webb, a local feminist who was slated to speak, remembers thinking, "Holy God, how did I get here?" Webb was three sentences into "the mildest speech you can imagine," she said, when men in the audience began to shout, "Take her off the stage and fuck her!" and "Fuck her down a dark alley!" All the while, she recalled, "Shulie is on my right saying, 'Keep going!'" Firestone tried to speak next, but was drowned out by a howl of sexual epithets.

That evening, Webb and other members of her group gathered in her apartment. "Everyone in that room came to the conclusion that there had to be a separate movement," she said. (Webb later launched *Off Our Backs*, which became the longest-running radical-feminist newspaper, and she started one of the first women's-studies programs, at Goddard College.) Firestone finally got her say in a letter "to the Left," published ten days later in *The Guardian*, a radical weekly based in New York:

> We have more important things to do than to try to get you to come around. You will come around when you have to, because you need us more than we need you. ... The message being: Fuck off, left. You can examine

your navel by yourself from now on. We're starting our own movement.

In March 1969, Firestone organized the nation's first abortion speakout, at Judson Memorial Church, on Washington Square. She persuaded twelve women to talk about experiences that were then regarded as shameful secrets: contraceptive devices that failed, back-alley operations, the anguish of giving up a baby for adoption. The speak-out drew hundreds of people of both sexes, who listened to the women respectfully and applauded their testimony.

By then, the groups that Firestone had founded, and a host of offshoots, were making headlines with confrontational protests and street theater. They disrupted state abortion-law hearings in Albany; occupied restaurants that wouldn't serve "unescorted" women; conducted a "Burial of Traditional Womanhood," in Arlington National Cemetery (the deceased wore curlers); released dozens of white mice to wreak havoc at a bridal fair at Madison Square Garden; held an "ogle-in" on Wall Street, to dole out some payback to leering men; and, most notorious, hurled brassieres, high heels, pots and pans, copies of *Playboy*, and other "instruments of female torture" into a Freedom Trash Can at the Miss America pageant, in Atlantic City. When Firestone was fired from a waitressing job and her boss withheld her wages, feminists stormed the restaurant and made him pay her on the spot.

But the rapid mitosis of groups was as much an indication of problems as of promise. New York Radical Women died soon after the Counter-Inaugural, overwhelmed by an avalanche of converts and riven with internal disagreements. Its successor organization, the Redstockings—cofounded by Firestone and Ellen Willis, then a writer for *The Village Voice* and *The New Yorker*—collapsed amid divisions over the role of consciousness-raising and accusations that Firestone and Willis were "dominating" meetings and, after they were quoted in *The Guardian*, "hoarding" attention. In late 1969, Firestone, with Anne Koedt, cofounded an organization that she hoped would circumvent these issues. Koedt drafted the founding statement, and Firestone wrote the organizational manifesto, in which she devised the structure for what became New York Radical Feminists, an organization made up of small "brigades." After an initial six-month period, in which members would steep themselves in feminist history and carry out a feminist action, a brigade would apply for formal recognition in the larger organization and start "seeding" new cadres. Each brigade would name itself after a historical feminist, and write a biographical booklet about its namesake. "We are committed to a flexible, non-dogmatic approach," Firestone wrote. "WE DO WHAT WORKS."

In April 1976, *Ms.* ran an essay that generated more letters than any article it had previously published. The author was Jo Freeman, and the subject was one that she had avoided committing to print for a long time: a "social disease" that had been attacking the women's movement for some years. She called it "trashing." She wrote:

> Like a cancer, the attacks spread from those who had reputations to those who were merely strong; from those who were active to those who merely had ideas; from those who stood out as individuals to those who failed to conform rapidly enough to the twists and turns of the changing line.

"Trashing" had surfaced in New York Radical Women just weeks after the group's founding. In a letter to Laya, Firestone wrote that several women had drawn up a statement against her, Anne Koedt, and Kathie Sarachild, an early member of the group, "for being a divisive faction," and "attacked me for being 'defensive' and 'unsisterly.'" The women voted to eject Firestone from the group. Another member, Anne Forer, objected. "I said, 'We have to have Shulie. There would be no women's liberation movement without her.'" The vote was dropped.

In Washington, DC, Marilyn Webb was forced out of *Off Our Backs*—*because* she was the only one with journalistic experience. "First it was 'You can't write at all; you have to help other people,'" she recalled. Then she was told that she couldn't accept public-speaking engagements. "And then it was just 'Get out!'" Freeman was ostracized by members of Westside, the group she had helped found. "There were dark hints about my 'male' ambitions—such as going to graduate school," she said. Carol Giardina, who now teaches women's studies and American history at Queens College, said, "I don't know anyone who founded a group and did early organizing" who wasn't thrown out. "It was just a disaster, a total disaster." She was ousted from her Florida group by "moon goddess" worshippers who accused her of being "too male-identified."

Anselma Dell'Olio, the founder of the New Feminist Theatre, in New York, was the first to speak publicly about trashing. In a 1970 address, titled "Divisiveness and Self-Destruction in the Women's Movement: A Letter of Resignation," which was delivered to the Congress to Unite Women, in New York City, she warned that women's "rage, masquerading as a pseudo-egalitarian radicalism under the 'pro-woman' banner," was turning into "frighteningly vicious anti-intellectual fascism of the left." After hearing about the speech, several women, including Freeman, met and vowed to fight the problem. "Instead, each of us slipped back into our own isolation," Freeman said. "The result was that most of the women at that meeting dropped out, as I had done. Two ended up in the hospital with nervous breakdowns." After Ti-Grace Atkinson resigned from the Feminists, a group she had founded in New York, she declared, "Sisterhood is power-ful. It kills. Mostly sisters." The observation rang true for so many that it soon became one of the lines most frequently quoted by feminists, or, rather, misquoted: the "mostly" was dropped.

Firestone and Koedt named New York Radical Feminists' first cadre the Stanton-Anthony Brigade, after Elizabeth Cady Stanton and Susan B. Anthony. Clues to the group's fate lie in the chronicle of another brigade, the West Village-1, which named itself not for a feminist forebear but for its neighborhood. The unofficial leader was Susan Brownmiller, a *Village Voice* writer. The partial minutes of the brigade's 1970 meetings are in Brownmiller's papers, at Harvard's Schlesinger Library:

> Feb. 1, 1970: A motion passed: "All actions initiated by 'our' group and totally carried out by us, should be credited to our name and not identified with the greater group as a whole."

> Feb. 8: Vote taken on whether to "split" the brigade in half. (6 yeas, 5 nays, 3 undecided).

> Feb. 15: Last week's debate to divide the group causing "upset" and "raised questions about passivity in women and their capacity to deal with power."

> March 8: Agenda item: "Abolition of the name 'Stanton-Anthony Brigade'—why should they have the name of two well known feminists?"

March 29: "Discussion of N.Y. Radical Feminist Manifesto—bring up point at large Group Meeting, to revise the manifesto."

Rancor toward the Stanton-Anthony brigade began building almost from the start. Firestone's tendency to be dismissive of others' grievances didn't help, nor did her intensity. At a famous demonstration in which a hundred women rallied at the *Ladies' Home Journal* offices to protest the publication's sexist content and hiring practices, Firestone jumped on the desk of the editor in chief, John Mack Carter, and tore up copies of the magazine in his face. Her detractors accused her of homicidal tendencies.

"The group is falling apart," Firestone wrote to Laya on May 26, 1970, and confessed to "a little bit of a sleepless night." She added, "Basically, I don't believe finally that the revolution is so imminent that it's worth tampering with my whole psychological structure, submitting to mob rule, and so on, which is what they're all into." Some days later, the members of New York Radical Feminists gathered in a hall downtown for a general meeting. The West Village-1 group aired its complaints, women began shouting at one another, and then they voted overwhelmingly to abolish the structure that Firestone had crafted. The Stanton-Anthony brigade retreated to the cellar, where Firestone and Koedt announced their resignations and left the hall. All but two of the Stanton-Anthony members quit soon thereafter, and Koedt withdrew from activism. "I was done with groups after that," she told me.

Brownmiller declined to talk to me about the incident, referring me to her memoir, *In Our Time* (1999), which claims only that Firestone "abruptly quit her fourth creation, New York Radical Feminists, after a split over leadership inside her Stanton-Anthony brigade." John Duff, a sculptor who was Firestone's on-again, off-again boyfriend in this period, remembers Firestone telling him that she had been forced out by an "antileadership" faction. "And guess who became the new leaders?" she said to him. "The antileaders." Late on the night of the vote, Firestone showed up at Anne Forer's door. Forer remembers her saying, "They threw me out and that's it."

* * *

The dissolution of New York Radical Feminists coincided with the movement's first mainstream publishing successes. Kate Millett's *Sexual Politics*, Firestone's *Dialectic*, and *Sisterhood Is Powerful*, an anthology edited by Robin Morgan, all sold well and were widely covered by the media. (Millett was on the cover of *Time*.) But, by the time *Dialectic* appeared in bookstores, in October 1970, Firestone was half a year into her self-exile from the movement. In the copy she sent to Laya, she wrote, "To Laya, the only true sister, after all."

Brownmiller wrote in her memoir that Firestone wanted her book to "place her in the firmament next to Simone de Beauvoir. She watched the media circus engulfing Kate and champed at the bit, awaiting her turn." Others recall the opposite. Firestone had already been denounced by feminists for violating the "We're all equals" ethic by accepting a book advance—of less than two thousand dollars—and for appearing on *The David Susskind Show*. James Landis, Firestone's editor at William Morrow, remembers with amazement that "she came to me quite troubled and said that the women in whatever group it was wanted to own the copyright. I told her, 'Forget it!'"

Instead, at the last minute, she slowed the book's production with a flurry of small corrections. She explained why in her roman à clef: "She thought of Anne Moffitt"—her pseudonym for Millett—"as a decoy, to deflect the klieg light." Her fears proved to be founded. The attention accorded the publication of *Sexual Politics* provoked an instant backlash within the movement as well as outside it. The emerging lesbian wing browbeat Millett into revealing that she was bisexual, and then denounced her for not having revealed it earlier. Millett had a breakdown and was committed to a mental hospital. In *Flying* (1974), she recalls a dream she had at the time, in which "figures of women ranged about a room question and cut at my life."

Meanwhile, *Dialectic* was stoking a small revolution at the Morrow offices. The female employees began asking questions: Why were all the secretaries and publicists women? Why were the few female editors underpaid? "We started having lunchtime meetings behind closed doors," Sara Pyle, an assistant in the publicity department at the time, told me. "We all stopped wearing our little heels and skirts." What made the women at Morrow "go a bit nuts," Pyle said, was the book's unvarnished radicalism. "Firestone took Marx further and put women in the picture," she said. "This was our oppression, all laid out." And not just women's oppression. The book's longest chapter, "Down with Childhood," chronicled the ways that children's lives had become constrained and regulated in modern society. "With the increase and exaggeration of children's dependence, woman's bondage to motherhood was also extended to its limits," Firestone wrote. "Women and children were now in the same lousy boat." The argument drew the appreciation of one notable feminist, which must have pleased Firestone. Simone de Beauvoir told *Ms.* that only Firestone "has suggested something new," noting how the book "associates Women's Liberation with children's liberation."

The liberator for Firestone was the right to be loved for oneself, not as part of a patronage system "to pass on power and privilege." She was trying to imagine a "home" where "all relationships would be based on love alone," a world, to paraphrase the last words of the book, that allows love to flow unimpeded. When *Dialectic* was published,

Firestone's sister Tirzah said, their father called it "the joke book of the century," and refused to read it.

* * *

In 1970, in a contribution to *Notes from the Second Year*, titled "Woman and Her Mind," Meredith Tax argued that the condition of women constituted a state of "female schizophrenia"—a realm of unreality where a woman either belonged to a man or was "nowhere, disappeared, teetering on the edge of a void with no work to do and no felt identity at all." By midcentury, Elaine Showalter noted, in *The Female Malady* (1985), scores of literary and journalistic works had defined schizophrenia as a "bitter metaphor" for the "cultural situation" of women. It was this state of affairs that the radical feminists had set out to change, only to find themselves doubly alienated. The first alienation was a by-product of their political vision: radical insight can resemble the mindset described by the clinical psychologist Louis Sass, in *Madness and Modernism* (1992), when he wrote that the schizophrenic is "acutely aware of the inauthenticities and compromises of normal social existence." The second alienation was tragic: alienation from one another.

Medical researchers have long puzzled over schizo-phrenia's late emergence (it was first diagnosed in 1911, in Switzerland) and its prevalence in the industrial world, where the illness is degenerative and permanent. (In "primitive" societies, when it exists at all, it is typically a passing malady.) In 2005, when Jean-Paul Selten and Elizabeth Cantor-Graae, experts on the epidemiology of schizophrenia, reviewed various risk factors—foremost among them migration, racism, and urban upbringing— they found that the factors all involved chronic isolation and loneliness, a condition that they called "social defeat." They theorized that "social support protects against the development of schizophrenia."

The second-wave feminists had hoped to alleviate this isolation through the refuge of sisterhood. "We were like pioneers who'd left the Old Country," Phyllis Chesler, a feminist psychologist and the author of *Women and Madness* (1972), told me. "And we had nowhere to go back to. We had only each other." That is, until the movement's collapse. Last fall, as I interviewed New York's founding radical feminists, the stories of "social defeat" mounted: painful solitude, poverty, infirmity, mental illness, and even homelessness. In a 1998 essay, "The Feminist Time Forgot," Kate Millett lamented the lengthening list of her sisters who had "disappeared to struggle alone in makeshift oblivion or vanished into asylums and have yet to return to tell the tale," or who fell into "despairs that could only end in death." She noted the suicides of Ellen Frankfort, the author of *Vaginal Politics*, and Elizabeth Fisher, the founder of *Aphra*, the first feminist literary journal. "We haven't helped each other much," Millett concluded. We "haven't been able to build solidly enough to have created community or safety."

* * *

By the time *Dialectic* came out, Firestone's life was in severe disarray. The coup within New York Radical Feminists was "totally devastating to her," Dell'Olio, one of the few feminists Firestone was still speaking to at the end of 1970, said. "It was like she'd been rejected by her family." She had begun work on an ambitious multimedia project that she described as a "female *Whole Earth Catalogue*." John Simon, an editor at Random House who discussed it with her, recalled, "You had the impression that there was something going on that was really complicated and deep and thoughtful," but, ultimately, "you couldn't make any sense of it."

Sometimes Firestone hid in plain sight. Her friend Robert Roth, the editor of the literary magazine *And Then*, recalled her wandering the East Village in disguise—sporting odd clothes and hairdos, and calling herself Kathy. Sometimes she kept far out of sight. She took a summer fellowship at an art school in Nova Scotia, where she tried, unsuccessfully, to work on the multimedia project, and then lived, for a time, in Cambridge, Massachusetts, where she worked, unrecognized, as a typist at MIT. John Duff recalled visiting her in the early seventies at her Tenth Street apartment and "this cockroach was walking across her desk. She went to crush it, and its guts smeared out in this really grotesque awful mess. And her remark? 'That's the story of my life.'"

It's unclear when the first symptoms of schizophrenia surfaced, but the decisive episode in its onset was a family crisis. In May 1974, Firestone was summoned home to St. Louis, with the news that her brother Daniel, then thirty, had died in a car crash. "It took me over twenty-four hours to dig out of my father the bitter truth that the body had a bullet hole in the chest," she wrote in *Airless Spaces*.

In 1972, Daniel had left the family faith, quit a job at the University of Missouri–St. Louis, where he had been teaching classics, and joined a Zen monastery in Rochester, New York. Two years later, he drove to a desolate area of New Mexico, made a makeshift Buddhist shrine, and shot himself in the heart, a fact not revealed until after he was buried with full Orthodox rites, a privilege that is denied in the case of suicide. Firestone refused to attend the funeral. She wrote that her brother's death, "whether murder or suicide, afterlife or no, contributed to my own growing madness."

In 1977, Sol and Kate Firestone announced that they were moving to Israel, and Shulamith flew to St. Louis to collect her paintings from the house. "Shulie and my father got into it again," Laya said, and Sol threatened to cut her out of his will. Some weeks later, he received a certified letter from Shulamith, disowning him first. Laya and Tirzah still have copies of a letter that their sister sent at the same time, to Kate. It was titled "Last Letter to My Mother" and finished with a jeremiad:

> When I see that in the final analysis, you are his, not His (let alone Hers); that you will let your loyalty to Sol (or even to his death), rule you (to the bitter end); that you have never made a serious attempt to govern your own life, (seizing it if necessary) but instead choose to go down with him (complaining all the way)—then … I can afford no pity for the maternal sufferings you (continue to) bring on yourself.
>
> Be grateful that you will not have the madness of this daughter as well to atone, for hereby I DISSOLVE MY TIES OF BLOOD.

Sol died, of congestive heart failure, in 1981, at the age of sixty-five. (Kate, who has Alzheimer's, still lives in Israel.) Laya had to send friends to Shulamith's apartment to get her to call, and, when she finally did, she was "ranting delusional stuff about how we were all part of a big conspiracy." Tirzah told me, "It was when our father died that Shulie went into psychosis. She lost that ballast he somehow provided."

In early 1987, Firestone's landlord on Second Street called Laya to say that the situation had become "dire." Neighbors were complaining that Firestone was screaming in the night and that she had left the taps running until the floorboards gave way. Laya flew to New York and found Shulamith emaciated and panhandling, carrying a bag holding a hammer and an unopened can of food. In the roman à clef, Firestone wrote that she had not eaten for a month—fearing that her food had been poisoned—and "looked like something out of Dostoevsky (which actually helped her beggar's earnings)." The next day, Laya took the action for which, she said, "Shulie never forgave me," and brought her to the Payne Whitney Clinic for evaluation. Her condition was diagnosed as paranoid schizophrenia, and she was involuntarily transferred to a residential facility in White Plains. "I am in deepest despair with no movement possible in any direction," Firestone wrote to Laya some weeks later. "Do not rest assured. Things are not O.K." On the back of the page, she scrawled in red ink, "Are you even on my side? Are you on your own side?"

The first hospitalization lasted nearly five months. During the next several years, Firestone was repeatedly hospitalized, at Beth Israel Medical Center. Her care generally fell to Dr. Margaret Fraser, a young psychiatrist. Fraser was struck by Firestone's "obvious" intelligence and her ability to speak coherently even in the midst of a psychotic break. She also recalled that Firestone suffered from a particularly insidious form of Capgras syndrome, the belief that people are hiding their identities behind masks: Firestone believed that people were hiding behind "masks of their own faces."

In 1989, a local newspaper ran a small gossipy item about how the author of *The Dialectic of Sex* was acting crazy and was about to be evicted from her Second Street studio. Kathie Sarachild, Ti-Grace Atkinson, Kate Millett, and a few others organized the Friends of Shulamith Firestone to fight the eviction in housing court. But Firestone, convinced that a member of her former cohort had placed the gossip item, wouldn't let them represent her.

In an anguished letter sent to the other members of the group the day after Christmas in 1989, Sarachild wrote that "none of us have been able to fulfill to our satisfaction any of our obligations as friends, neighbors, admirers and old political 'co-conspirators,'" and that Firestone may now be "in greater danger of homelessness and starvation than when we began." Two weeks later, Millett sent a letter to Firestone. She wrote, "Please get your act together and take an interest. Get with it. You have a hell of a lot to lose and burying your head in the sand isn't going to help." Firestone didn't reply. She was ultimately evicted from the studio, her art consigned to the trash.

* * *

A second effort to convene a support system was more successful. Starting in the early nineties, and under the supervision of Margaret Fraser, a group of women met weekly with Firestone to help her with practical needs, from taking her antipsychotic medications to buying groceries. The composition of the group fluctuated, but the most dedicated members were a few young women who had studied her writings, and Lourdes Cintron, a caseworker from the Visiting Nurse Service of New York, who had been inspired by *Dialectic* in her youth as a pro-independence activist in Puerto Rico. The service didn't want Firestone as a client—she had no health insurance—but Cintron insisted. "I said to my supervisor, 'Look, this is a woman who did so much for women,'" she recalled, "'and now she's going to be abandoned by women?'" A nearly decade-long friendship began. Firestone dedicated *Airless Spaces* to Cintron.

The periods between hospitalizations lengthened. After 1993, Firestone was going a year or more without relapse, helped by the medications and, especially, by the support of her new circle, including two young women who moved to New York to find her: Marisa Figueiredo, a physician's assistant who said that *Dialectic* had "changed my life" when she read it as a teenager in Akron, Ohio; and Lori Hiris, an aspiring filmmaker so galvanized by the book's "incredible clarity" that she came to Manhattan to make documentaries about radical feminism. Along with Beth Stryker, a new-media artist, and Lourdes López, a human-resources manager at Columbia University, they became mainstays in Firestone's life, taking her on trips to the country (on Hiris's motorcycle), helping her to adopt a cat (Pussy Firestone), and debating Beat poetry, classical music, and punk rock over the two-dollar Sunday egg special at a neighborhood dive. There was only one subject that Firestone wouldn't discuss, Hiris said: feminism. "It was the one conversation piece that you did not want to bring up."

"The support group is really proving its worth," Firestone wrote to Fraser in a New Year's Day card, in 1995. "I may be redeemed once again." At her young fans' urging, she had started writing *Airless Spaces*. The book opens with a dream: A woman is on a sinking luxury liner. While deluded merrymakers dance "like in a Grosz cartoon," she descends belowdecks seeking an "air pocket" and locks herself in a refrigerator, "hoping to live on even after the boat was fully submerged." Through autobiographical vignettes, Firestone describes a population of what she calls, with her usual directness, "losers," solitary exemplars of the state of "social defeat." Beth Stryker took the manuscript to an editor she knew at Semiotext(e), an avant-garde imprint, who accepted it at once. To celebrate the publication, in 1998, a group of Firestone's old colleagues turned out for a reading in an art gallery downtown. Several of them, including Kate Millett and Phyllis Chesler, did the actual reading; Firestone was too nervous. Chesler remembers her "hugging the wall, like a little wounded child, but also proud."

The recovery didn't last. By the late nineties, the support group had started to dissipate—Margaret Fraser moved, as did the psychiatrist who replaced her; Lourdes

Cintron fell ill; the younger women found jobs in other cities—and soon stopped meeting altogether. Firestone again began to be hospitalized repeatedly, ultimately in the gritty public ward of Bellevue Hospital. She withdrew into her old seclusion, not answering the phone or the door, not speaking even to Laya. One spurned visitor recalled that she heard a torrent of Hebrew coming from inside the apartment. Firestone was reciting Jewish prayers. When Laya came to New York a few years ago, and her sister finally answered the phone, she begged her to at least show her face. "I said, 'Shulie, I'm walking by your apartment. Just look out the window and I'll wave to you.'" She didn't.

On August 28 last year, after Firestone's rent bill had sat outside her door for several days, the landlord sent the building superintendent up the fire escape to peer in her window. He made out a still figure, face down on the floor. The police were summoned. A neighbor phoned Carol Giardina to tell her that Firestone's body had been found, and Giardina and Kathie Sarachild hurried to the apartment, to what end they weren't certain. At least, Sarachild remembered thinking, they could "make sure the door was locked" after the police left. When they arrived, the police told them to wait in the stairwell. After a while, Sarachild said, several officers emerged and the women watched them "going down those five flights of stairs, that little body in the bag."

* * *

Firestone was buried, in a traditional Orthodox funeral, in a Long Island cemetery, where her maternal grandparents are interred. Ten male relatives made up a minyan. None of her feminist comrades were invited. "At the end of the day, the old-time religion asserted itself," Tirzah said. Ezra gave a eulogy. He lives in Brooklyn, where he works as an insurance salesman, but he hadn't spoken to Shulamith in years, and he broke down several times as he told how she, more than anyone else in the family, had tended to him as a child and taught him compassion. He recalled a story she told him when he was a boy, about a man on a train who realized that he had dropped a glove on the platform and, as the train left the station, dropped the other glove from the window, so that someone could have a pair. Then he lamented Shulamith's "tragic" failure to make a "good marriage" and have children "who would be devoted to her."

When Tirzah's turn came to give a eulogy, she addressed Ezra. "I said to him, 'Excuse me, but with all due respect, Shulie was a model for Jewish women and girls everywhere, for women and girls everywhere. She had children—she influenced thousands of women to have new thoughts, to lead new lives. I am who I am, and a lot of women are who they are, because of Shulie.'"

Acknowledgments

I want to thank the following people for helping me with word processing, editing, proofreading, text design, and solicitation of publisher: Marisa Figueiredo, Jack Penrod, Chris Kraus, Ben Meyers, and Beth Stryker. Special thanks to Susan Kandel for making preparation of the manuscript possible.

ABOUT THE AUTHORS

Shulamith Firestone (1945–2012) was born in Ottawa, Canada, and grew up in St. Louis, MO. After receiving a BA from Washington University in St. Louis and a BFA from the Art Institute of Chicago, she moved to New York City. There she founded some of the first—and foremost—radical feminist organizations in the United States. In 1970, at the age of twenty-five, she published *The Dialectic of Sex*, one of the most widely discussed books of the second-wave feminist movement. Semiotext(e) published *Airless Spaces*, her second book, in 1998.

Susan Faludi is a Pulitzer Prize–winning journalist and the author of the bestselling *Backlash: The Undeclared War Against American Women*. Her most recent book, *In the Darkroom*, won the 2016 Kirkus Prize for Nonfiction.

Chris Kraus is a writer, critic, and co-editor of Semiotexte, alongside Hedi El Kholti. Her latest book is *The Four Spent the Day Together*, a novel forthcoming in 2025.